MEXICAN
family favorites
COOK BOOK

by

María Teresa Bermúdez

GOLDEN WEST
PUBLISHERS

Front and back cover artwork by Bruce Robert Fischer

Library of Congress Cataloging-in-Publication Data

Bermúdez, María Teresa
    Mexican family favorites cook book.

    Includes index.
    1. Cookery, Mexican. I. Title
TX716.M4B425 1983   641.5972   83-11692
ISBN 0-914846-17-5

Printed in the United States of America

17th Printing, © 1998

Information in this book is deemed to be authentic and accurate by author and publisher. However, they disclaim any liability incurred in connection with the use of information appearing in this book.

Golden West Publishers
4113 N. Longview Ave.
Phoenix, AZ 85014 USA

Golden West Publishers books are available at special discounts to schools, clubs, organizations and businesses for use as fund-raisers, premiums and special promotions. Send inquiry to director of Marketing.

Contents

Foreword

Mexican food is often imitated but nothing compares to authentic Mexican dishes, especially family favorites.

Mexican dishes are extremely versatile and individually scrumptious as well as rich in cultural heritage from both Indian and Spanish influences. The best recipes are the ones that stay closest to the original. Home recipes are everyone's favorite!

This book is a synthesis of recipes of a Southwestern Mexican-American family. The recipes featured are best loved and everyday dishes. These recipes are ones I've grown up with and are an ethnic aspect of my life.

I hope you enjoy *Mexican Family Favorites Cook Book* and learn to love its recipes as I do. One last recognition of gratitude goes to my mother who so generously offered her guidance and suggestions, not to mention the recipes which are an integral part of this book.

¡Buen provecho! Good appetite!

María Teresa Bermúdez

Basics of Mexican Cookery

To keep your Mexican dishes authentically delicious, here are some points:

Know Your Chiles

If you were asked to identify one characteristic that would singularly describe Mexican dishes, "chile" would be the answer, namely chile peppers. Whether ground, whole, sliced, diced, pickled, fresh, canned or dried, chile peppers are an inherent part of Mexican dishes!

There are many varieties of chiles, ranging from mild to very hot! Cooks use whatever chiles are available to them. Some varieties are available canned when they aren't available fresh. Here is a list of some common peppers.

GREEN PEPPERS or "bell" peppers are very mild peppers used in salads as a garnish and to flavor and color dishes.

ANAHEIM or "California" are mild, long, green chiles. They can be eaten raw and used in salads.

JALAPEÑOS, smaller sized dark green chiles, are very hot!

SERRANOS are smaller and slimmer than jalapeños, hotter too!

ANCHO chiles are plump dark green chiles that range from mild to medium hot. Ancho means "wide," that's why these are the best choice for chile rellenos!

YELLOW HOTS are longer than jalapeños and moderately hot. These chiles are used in hot mixes, along with other chiles and are used in salsas and as a garnish to color dishes.

WAX CHILES are small, slender, yellow chiles used in pickled mixes, in salsas and as garnish.

CHILITEPINS are tiny, seedy red peppers used for seasoning in salsas in combinations with other chiles. They are also used in pickling. They are *very, very hot!*

Chiles are used fresh or canned. There are two common ways to cook chiles, roasting or deep frying.

Roast chiles over top burner of your stove, turning frequently to keep chiles from burning. Three to four chiles can be done at a time. When skins turn dark brown and look blistered, remove from heat. Wrap chiles in a damp kitchen towel or paper towel to make skins easier to remove.

Chiles can be roasted in an oven. Place a baking sheet under chiles. Bake at 350 F until skins are brown and blistered. After roasting, wrap chiles in a damp kitchen towel for a few minutes, then remove skins.

In a deep fryer, cook chiles until they turn brown and look blistered. Drain on paper towels before removing skins.

Dried chiles are used to make various dishes and to make chili powder. Dried chiles can be purchased in grocery stores or you can dry your own.

To dry chiles, make a chile "garland." String chiles up by their stems to make a cluster. Let hang in a dry place until they become quite dry. Fresh green chiles turn from green to red when left to dry out. Dried chiles are ready to use when they are crackly-dry.

Chile garlands can be used decoratively in your kitchen, living room or patio. These *sartas* or *ristras* are a characteristic sight in the Southwest.

To use dried chiles, soak them in hot water until they are softened. Open chiles and remove stem and seeds. Puree chiles in a food processor or blender. Add small amount of water to process. If chiles are hot, add a water and vinegar mixture to help tame the chiles. When a chili paste is made, pass through a sieve to make a smooth paste. Season paste as desired to make salsas or for cooking.

Commercial chili powder can be used for making sauces for tacos or enchiladas, salsas and dishes like chili con carne. When using store-bought chili powder, check labels to see what spices are included. Pure-ground chili powder is available and you can add your own favorite spices and seasonings.

You can also make your own chili powder. Here is a homemade version.

Chili Powder

6 oz. dried CHILES (mild, hot or combinations)
2 Tbsp. ground CUMIN
2 tsp. ground PAPRIKA
4 tsp. SALT
2 tsp. GARLIC SALT
2 tsp. OREGANO
2 tsp. ONION SALT
2 tsp. fresh dried CILANTRO

Cut off stems of chiles with a knife. Blend all ingredients with chiles in a blender or food processor until powdery. Makes 2/3 cup of a zesty chili powder. Store in an air-tight glass jar.

To take the sting out of hot chili peppers, add vinegar to your hot salsa or soak chiles before using in equal parts of water and vinegar. Another way to tame hot chili peppers is to use combinations of chiles (mild and hot). Use green peppers (bell peppers) and a few hot chile peppers mixed together. Overly hot chile peppers in a dish can ruin a dinner, especially if your guests are not accustomed to the sting.

Tortillas

To Mexicans, tortillas are bread. If you know how to make tortillas you will be able to make more authentic enchiladas, tacos, etc. The flour tortilla and corn tortilla recipes in the **Panes** section of the book are simple-to-follow home-tried recipes which will make you an expert tortilla maker with a little practice!

There is nothing like the satisfaction derived from a new-found skill. Do try these two recipes. Children will also enjoy making tortillas.

When purchasing store-bought tortillas, look for smooth, soft-textured, fresh-looking flour tortillas and smooth, fairly pliable, even-textured corn tortillas.

Tortillas can be fried, eaten plain, baked, topped with sauces, served with jelly or any filling! Corn tortillas are made into nachos, used for tacos, flautas, enchiladas, etc. Mini corn or flour tortillas are good to serve as appetizers topped with your favorite toppings!

"Gorditas" are thicker flour tortillas popular in the Southwest. A dish of pinto beans and warmed, buttered gordita tortillas is a common tasty snack!

Side Dishes

Beans are another staple of life. Pinto and calico beans are the most common beans eaten, although there are other varieties. If you know how to fix a pot of pinto beans, you will be able to prepare all dishes calling for beans for authentic Mexican cooking! Alone, beans, especially refried beans, make a basic side dish.

Beans are mashed or creamed to fill tacos, burros, tostadas. As a side dish they can be served whole or mashed. Refried beans are mashed beans cooked in oil. Beans are high in protein and other nutrients. For the dieter, they are economical in calories.

Rice is another basic side dish to complement most Mexican dishes. "Mexican Rice" can be made in a variety of ways. Every Mexican household has its own version. The **Mexican Rice** recipe from this book is a family favorite. For a less starchy Mexican rice, soak rice in very hot water before cooking. When water has cooled enough to touch, rub rice through your fingers, then rinse and repeat. This process removes starch. Allow the rice to dry as completely as possible by spreading it on waxed paper. Then fry rice in shortening or vegetable oil.

Salsas

Salsas are used as dips, garnishes to top chalupas, tacos, burros, etc. Salsas can be made with green or red chile and they can be mild or hot depending on the chile you use. Salsas are very versatile!

Mole

"Mole" is a paste of chiles, spices, peanuts, cocoa or chocolate, bread crumbs or corn tortilla pieces. It is a thick, rich sauce which can vary in ingredients, resulting in many versions. Mole is used as a sauce for turkey, chicken, pork, roasts and fish. Stew the meat and make the mole using the meat stock. Then pour the mole over the meat and serve!

Mole can be purchased ready to use. You can also make your own mole.

Spices and Herbs

ANISE is the fruit of a small plant. The seed is used. The best is grown in Spain, Mexico and India.

BAY LEAF—from the laurel of sweet bay tree. It is an aromatic leaf. Used for meats, soups and pickles.

CAYENNE PEPPER—from a tropical shrub. The powdered pods and seeds of these shrubs are used. "Red Pepper" is another name for cayenne.

CHILE—a hot pepper used as a base for chile sauce. There are many different kinds with varying degrees of hotness.

CHILI POWDER is the combination of ground red peppers and spices. You can't substitute for chili powder if you're making Mexican dishes!

CHILITEPINS is the fruit and seed of a shrub that dries into small seedy pods. They are very, very hot and among the smallest of peppers. Chilitepins are minced and ground and used in meats and as a garnish. They are also used in salsas. Use 1 to 2 chilitepins to make hot salsa! Green chilitepins are used whole for pickling.

CORIANDER is an herb whose seeds are used for meats, pickles and desserts.

CUMIN—a spice used in chili powders for meats, sausages and pickles. It has a slightly tart taste and is a must for chorizo!

GARLIC comes from the lily family and is a very strong flavored herb. Garlic cloves are minced/ground used for stewing meats, fish, chicken and for salsas. Use in moderation. The truly best tasting dishes use a balance of spices and herbs. Too much garlic can ruin a dish while too little leaves a dish lacking in potential flavorfulness!

Garlic in Mexico is used medicinally as a cure-all. Garlic is said to ward off diseases of the mind and body. It is crushed and rubbed into the skin, boiled, eaten or swallowed whole by cloves. It is worn sometimes as part of a necklace. Older members in our family believe in garlic medicinally and spiritually while younger members do not. In Mexico, especially in smaller towns and villages and even to some Mexican families in the Southwest, garlic is considered a healing and preventative "talisman."

GARLIC SALT is a mixture of ground garlic and fine white salt.

OLIVE OIL, although not a spice or herb, merits a few words. We use olive oil often for dishes like paella. Olive oil comes from the flesh of ripe olives. "Virgin" oil, which is from the first extraction, is best.

ONION, from the lily family, has a strong flavor. Yellow Spanish onion is used most in our house.

ONION SALT, a dried mixture of onion and fine white salt, is used to flavor meats, salads and soups.

PAPRIKA is a sweet red pepper dried and ground after stem and seeds are removed.

PEPPER is made from peppercorns, the dried berries of the *piper nigrum* vine. **WHITE PEPPER** is made from what remains after the outer coat of a fully ripened berry is removed. **BLACK PEPPER** is made from the whole berry.

PIMIENTO is the fleshy fruit of the Spanish paprika.

THYME is an herb whose powdered dried leaves are used for meats, poultry and fish dishes.

Desayuno/Breakfast

Huevos y Chorizo
(Scrambled Eggs with Chorizo)

6 EGGS
¾ tsp. SALT
⅛ tsp. PEPPER
1/3 cup MILK
2 Tbsp. BUTTER
½ cup CHORIZO* (fresh or store bought)

In a bowl, beat eggs lightly. Add seasonings and milk. In a skillet, heat butter. Add chorizo and eggs and scramble. Cook over low heat, stir slowly. Do not allow eggs to become overly dry. (Serves 4-6) Serve with hot buttered flour tortillas.

*See recipe for **Chorizo**

Huevos con Papas y Chorizo
(Eggs, Potatoes, Sausage)

3 medium-sized baking POTATOES, peeled, diced
3 to 4 Tbsp. BACON FAT or oil
½ lb. CHORIZO
SALT to taste
¼ tsp. coarsely ground PEPPER
½ tsp. coarsely ground OREGANO
5 well-beaten EGGS

Rinse diced potatoes in colander. In a skillet, heat fat or oil, then add well-drained diced potatoes and cook over medium heat, covered, until tender-firm. Stir frequently to keep from sticking.

In a fry pan, while potatoes are cooking, cook chorizo, and when well-cooked, drain thoroughly. Put in bowl and leave nearby.

When potatoes are tender-firm, season with salt, pepper, and oregano. Cook until tender. In a bowl, beat eggs well and cook in the fry pan used for making chorizo. When eggs are cooked, place in large bowl and sprinkle in chorizo. Blend well. Mix in potatoes.

Serve immediately. (Serves 4-5)

Chorizo (Sausage)

Chorizo is Mexican sausage. It can be prepared and stored uncooked or cooked until you are ready to use it. Uncooked chorizo can be freezer kept quite well! Tacos with chorizo filling are very tasty!

1 lb. well-ground BEEF
½ lb. well-ground PORK
1 minced GARLIC CLOVE
½ small ONION, finely diced
3 Tbsp. VINEGAR

2½ Tbsp. CHILI POWDER*
½ tsp. PAPRIKA
¼ tsp. BLACK PEPPER
¼ tsp. CLOVES
1 tsp. SALT

1 tsp. OREGANO
2 finely crushed CHILITEPINS**

To ground beef and pork, blend in minced garlic clove and onions. In a bowl, add vinegar and dissolve chili powder. Add seasonings and chilitepins, mix well. Add this to meat mixture, blend in thoroughly. Form into a roll and place in an airtight bag, refrigerate until ready to use. To use, simply cook desired amount of chorizo over medium heat until chorizo turns a richer brown color and meat is fully cooked. Drain and use!

*Check to make sure the chili powder has cumin. This seasoning gives chorizo its subtly tart flavor.
**Chilitepins are tiny hot peppers which give the chorizo its scotiness. Use only two. They go a long way! When working with chilitepins, wash hands thoroughly and avoid touching eyes.

Torta de Chorizo (Sausage Omelet)

Use store bought chorizo or your own chorizo!

6 EGGS, separated
6 Tbsp. HOT WATER
¾ tsp. SALT
1½ Tbsp. BUTTER
2/3 cup CHORIZO, cooked

In a bowl, beat egg yolks vigorously. Add water and seasonings, mix well. Beat egg whites until stiff. Add egg yolks to egg whites.
In a skillet or omelet pan, melt butter. Add egg mixture into pan and cook over low heat until omelet is light brown and top is dry. Add chorizo, then fold omelet over. Serve immediately! (Serves 6)

Papas y Chorizo (Potatoes and Sausage)

3 large baking POTATOES, peeled
3 to 4 Tbsp. OIL for frying
½ lb. CHORIZO
pinch OREGANO

Dice potatoes and rinse thoroughly. In a skillet, heat safflower oil, peanut oil or salad oil. When oil is hot, add potatoes, cover and cook over medium heat. Stir occasionally.

In a fry pan, cook chorizo. Chorizo should always be well-cooked. Chorizo takes on a dark reddish color when cooked. Mash chorizo and stir frequently during cooking. When chorizo is cooked, drain.

Season potatoes with salt and pepper as desired. When potatoes are tender, add drained chorizo and blend in well. Add a pinch of oregano and cover to simmer 10 minutes. Serve hot with eggs or as burritos! (Serves 4-5)

Huevos con Chile Verde
(Eggs with Green Chiles)

This recipe for scrambled egg and green chiles is very popular in my house. Try it with jalapeño if you like hot chile! Serve with salsa and warm tortillas.

2 Tbsp. BUTTER or margarine
2 Tbsp. chopped ONIONS
4 oz. can diced GREEN CHILES (or fresh chiles, cooked or raw)
1 TOMATO, diced
½ tsp. SALT
¼ tsp. GARLIC POWDER
PEPPER to taste
6 EGGS, well-beaten
dash PAPRIKA

Saute onions and chiles (if you use raw chiles) in butter until tender. Add diced chiles if you used canned chiles and mix in with tomato. Add seasonings and let simmer for a few minutes. Beat eggs until creamy and add to chile mixture. Cook eggs, sprinkle with paprika. (Serves 4)

Huevos Rancheros #1 (Ranch Eggs)

2 Tbsp. chopped ONIONS
2 Tbsp. chopped GREEN PEPPERS
2 Tbsp. BUTTER
½ lb. chopped, cooked BEEF
½ tsp. SALT
⅛ tsp. PEPPER
⅛ tsp. PAPRIKA
⅛ tsp. GARLIC POWDER
4 EGGS
OIL for cooking

Saute onions and green peppers in butter until both are tender. Mix in meat and seasonings. Let simmer, covered.

In a bowl, beat eggs thoroughly and pour into a hot, well-oiled skillet, then add meat mixture evenly over the eggs. Brown both sides. (Serves 4-5)

Serve with salsa, sliced green chiles, sliced tomatoes or avocados, and warm, buttered corn or flour tortillas.

Huevos con Jamón y Chiles (Eggs with Ham and Chiles)

2 tsp. VEGETABLE OIL
1 Tbsp. diced ONION
4-oz. can diced GREEN CHILES
¾ cup cooked diced HAM
6 large EGGS
¾ tsp. SALT
¼ tsp. PEPPER

In a skillet, heat oil and saute onions until tender. Add chiles and ham. Cook until well heated. Beat eggs and sprinkle in salt and pepper. Pour eggs into skillet and scramble over medium heat. Serve warm. (Serves 5-6)

Burrito de Huevo, Jamón y Chiles

For Ham and Chile Egg burritos, fix eggs as in the previous recipe. Scramble eggs loosely and do not allow them to become too dry. Warm 4-5 flour tortillas. When eggs are cooked, fill equal amounts of egg mixture in each tortilla. Roll tortillas up and tuck one end. Serve with salsa. (Serves 4-5)

Huevos Rancheros #2 (Ranch Eggs)

Here is a meatless version. Serve with its own salsa!

8 Tbsp. OIL
8 mini CORN TORTILLAS
8 EGGS
SALSA
½ cup shredded CHEESE

Heat oil and soften corn tortillas on both sides by dipping them in hot oil. Drain and set aside in a warmer. Fry eggs sunny-side-up, then place eggs over corn tortillas. Top with salsa and garnish with cheese. Serve two per serving. (Serves 4)

Salsa

4 to 5 stewed TOMATOES
1 to 2 Tbsp. diced ONION
1 tsp. OIL
SALT to taste
GARLIC SALT to taste
4-oz. can drained, diced GREEN CHILES

Chop the tomatoes and combine with onion. Heat in a saucepan with oil and salt. Cook over medium heat until well blended. Mix in drained chiles and cover to simmer. Serve hot over **Huevos Rancheros.**

Burrito de Huevo (Egg Burrito)

6 EGGS
¾ tsp. SALT
⅛ tsp. PEPPER
3 to 4 Tbsp. EVAPORATED MILK
2 Tbsp. BUTTER
6 flour TORTILLAS (12-inch size)

In a bowl, mix eggs and seasonings, beat lightly. Add milk, blend well. Add butter to skillet and melt, then add eggs. Scramble eggs lightly.

When eggs are cooked, warm tortillas and add egg in each one and roll into a burrito. Add cheese, chili, chorizo, meat to eggs. Serve with salsa. (Serves 6)

Huevos Revueltos (Scrambled Eggs)

This chile and scrambled egg dish goes well with a tasty bowl of menudo! Serve with warmed flour tortillas!

OIL to saute onions
5 Tbsp. diced ONION
2 chopped GREEN CHILES, fresh
5 EGGS
SALT/PEPPER to taste
shredded CHEESE as garnish

Heat salad oil or peanut oil. Saute onions, then add chopped green chiles and cook for a few minutes. Whip eggs to a creamy texture, then add to chile mixture and cook eggs. Serve and top with shredded cheese. (Serves 4)

Fiesta Souffle

½ cup RICOTTA CHEESE
1 tsp. OREGANO
1 tsp. DRY MUSTARD
dash CAYENNE PEPPER
3 oz. PARMESAN CHEESE, grated
4 Tbsp. MILK
8 oz. cream-style CORN
½ cup chopped PIMIENTOS
3 EGGS, separated
SALT

Preheat oven to 400 F. In a mixing bowl, combine ricotta cheese, oregano, dry mustard, pepper and Parmesan cheese. Add milk, corn, pimientos and egg yolks. Mix well.

In a separate bowl, whip egg whites with a pinch of salt. Egg whites should be stiff but not dry. Fold egg whites into cheese batter. Butter 6 custard dishes and spoon batter into each dish. Place dishes in pan filled with hot water approximately 2/3 way up sides of custard dishes.

Bake for 15-20 minutes, until souffles are golden brown. Centers should be soft. Makes 6 individual **Fiesta Souffles!**

Torta de Chile Verde
(Green Chile Omelet)

Another delicious omelet is one with green chiles as the "filling."

6 EGGS
6 Tbsp. HOT WATER
¾ tsp. SALT
dash PEPPER
¼ tsp. PAPRIKA
BUTTER for cooking
2 seeded, sliced fresh GREEN CHILES (or canned chiles)
½ cup shredded CHEDDAR CHEESE

In a bowl, separate eggs. Place egg whites in a smaller bowl or dish. Beat egg yolks thoroughly. Add water, seasonings, mix well. Beat egg whites until stiff. Add egg whites to yolks, blend well.

In a skillet or omelet pan, melt butter. Add egg mixture and cook. When omelet is dry on top and brown, add chiles and fold-over. Then add shredded cheddar cheese, and allow cheese to melt. Serve with salsa. (Serves 6)

Torta de Nopal (Cactus Omelet)

6 EGGS, separated
6 Tbsp. MILK
¼ tsp. SALT
¾ cup diced cooked NOPAL
2 Tbsp. diced cooked GREEN CHILES
1 fresh medium TOMATO, peeled, chopped
1 tsp. crushed fresh dried CILANTRO
SALT to taste
2 Tbsp. BUTTER

Beat egg whites until stiff. Beat egg yolks until creamy. Add milk and salt. Combine yolks to white and mix briefly.

In a bowl, mix nopal, green chiles, tomato and seasonings, turn into a sauce pan and cook in 1 teaspoon vegetable oil, for a few minutes.

Cook eggs in 2 tablespoons butter in a skillet or omelet pan until top is dry. Add filling and fold omelet over. Press to seal and cook until well heated but not dry. Serve with salsa. (Serves 4-5)

Torta de Aguacate y Jamón (Avocado and Ham Omelet)

6 EGGS, separated
6 Tbsp. MILK
½ tsp. SALT
¼ tsp. PEPPER
2 Tbsp. BUTTER

In a bowl, beat egg whites until stiff. In a separate bowl, beat yolks thoroughly. Add milk, salt and pepper. Fold in egg whites.

Heat oven to 325 F, lightly grease a baking sheet.

In a skillet or omelet pan, heat butter then pour in egg mixture. Cook omelet until bottom is golden brown.* Transfer omelet into greased baking sheet and bake until top is fully cooked. Add part of the filling and fold over omelet, then add rest of filling over omelet and bake in oven until filling is fully heated. (Serves 4)

*While omelet is cooking, make omelet filling!

Filling

1 cup SOUR CREAM
1 tsp. SALT
¼ tsp. PAPRIKA
1 TOMATO, diced, peeled
1 medium-sized ripe AVOCADO, diced
½ cup cooked HAM, diced

In a sauce pan, heat sour cream, add seasonings. Add tomato, avocado and ham, blend in well. Cover, set aside away from heat.

Huevos con Tortilla Fritas

This egg and corn tortilla hash makes a tasty breakfast dish.

OIL for frying
5 to 6 CORN TORTILLAS, cut into small pieces
6 large EGGS, well beaten in 1 Tbsp. MILK
¾ tsp. SALT
⅛ tsp. PEPPER

Heat oil in a skillet and brown corn tortilla pieces until slightly crispy. Add salt and pepper in bowl with eggs and milk, mix. Pour egg mixture into skillet with tortillas and cook over low heat until eggs are cooked. (Serves 5-6)

Torta de Camaron (Shrimp Omelet)

6 EGGS (separated)   dash PEPPER
6 Tbsp. HOT WATER   dash PAPRIKA
¾ tsp. SALT   1½ Tbsp. BUTTER

Beat egg whites until stiff but not dry and set aside. Beat egg yolks until thick, then add water. Beat, add seasonings, mix well. Fold yolks and stiff egg whites together. Melt butter in omelet pan. Make sure pan is well-greased. Turn egg mixture into pan, cover and cook over low heat until puffy. Cook omelet uncovered until top is dry and light brown. Before folding over omelet, add shrimp filling. Fold over omelet, pressing lightly to seal. (Serves 6)

Shrimp filling can be made while omelet is in pan.

Shrimp Filling

1 tsp. MARGARINE
1/3 cup grated CHEESE
SALT/PEPPER to taste
¾ oz. finely ground SHRIMP

Melt margarine and cheese in sauce pan, add salt and pepper to taste, add shrimp, stir well, heat to a boil. When cheese is melted, it is ready for omelet.

Nopales con Huevos Revueltos (Eggs with Prickly Pear)

OIL for frying
chopped ONIONS
¼ cup PIMIENTOS
6 EGGS
⅛ tsp. OREGANO
¼ tsp. coarsely ground PEPPER
¾ cup diced NOPALES
SALT to taste
CHEESE or SALSA as garnish

Heat oil and saute onions and pimientos. Beat eggs until creamy, add to onions and pimientos and cook. Season with oregano and pepper. Add diced nopales and cook long enough to fully heat them. Salt to taste. Serve at once. Garnish with shredded cheese or salsa as desired. (Serves 5)

Mexican Cheese Souffle

As a dinner or breakfast entree this cheese souffle topped with its own cheese/pimiento sauce is delicious!

1½ cups MILK + 1/3 cup EVAPORATED MILK
6 EGGS, separated
1¼ cups BUTTER
1 small, well-chopped GREEN PEPPER
¼ cup FLOUR
1 tsp. SALT
½ tsp. CAYENNE PEPPER
dash PAPRIKA
½ lb. shredded, sharp CHEDDAR CHEESE
4-oz. can diced GREEN CHILES
2 diced JALAPEÑO CHILES

Heat oven to 315 F. Heat milk in sauce pan. Place egg whites in large bowl and egg yolks in small bowl. Melt butter and quickly saute chopped green peppers. Then add flour, stir, add this to heated milk. Add salt, cayenne pepper, paprika. Cook until smooth and thick; stir constantly. Add cheese and stir until smooth; cook until cheese is melted. Remove from heat and set aside.

Beat egg yolks with fork until well blended. Stir into cheese mixture. Add to this canned green chiles and jalapeño chiles. Mix well. Beat egg whites until stiff, not dry. Slowly pour cheese/yolk mixture into bowl with egg whites, fold in. Pour mixture into ungreased 2-quart souffle dish. With the end of a knife make a shallow indentation in the souffle all around to form crown. Bake at 315 F for 1 hour and 10 minutes or until souffle is fluffy and browned. Don't open oven door while souffle is baking, but it's okay to take a peek during last 20 minutes of baking time. Serve souffle with cheese/pimiento sauce. (Serves 4)

Cheese/Pimiento Sauce

2 Tbsp. melted BUTTER
1 Tbsp. FLOUR
1 cup MILK + 2 Tbsp. EVAPORATED MILK
dash SALT and PEPPER
3 Tbsp. diced PIMIENTOS
1 cup shredded CHEDDAR CHEESE

Blend butter and flour, add milk and boil until thick. Add salt, pepper and pimientos. Stir, then add cheese. Continue to heat until cheese is completely melted. (Makes 2 cups sauce)

Panes/Breads

Corn Tortillas

Indians ground their own corn on stone to make their corn tortillas. These tortillas were thick and were used as bread. They were a basic food staple. Today, making tortillas is an infinitely easier process, since we can purchase corn flour. Corn tortillas have become thinner and many Mexican people still consider them "bread."

> **2 cups CORN FLOUR (Masa Harina)**
> **¾ tsp. SALT**
> **1 cup WATER + a little more, if necessary**

In a bowl, add flour and salt and mix very well. Then add water, a little at a time while mixing. Take dough in hands and form into an elastic dough. Knead thoroughly, add more water, if necessary to keep dough moist. Dough should hold its shape but still be moist.

Form 12 dough balls. Take 2 sheets of waxed paper and place one dough ball in the center. Press down and flatten dough; use a small plate. Make a thin tortilla 6 inches around. Cook on an ungreased griddle, leaving the top sheet of waxed paper on the tortilla. Cook until the edges of the tortilla turn brown and small air bubbles stop forming. Remove second sheet of waxed paper, turn tortilla and cook. Do the same with all dough balls.

Allow tortillas to cool, then place in plastic bag and refrigerate. (Makes 12)

Tortilla Snack

Take a corn tortilla, warm it, and dab with your favorite jam. Cream cheese or any melted cheese tastes great and makes a quick, nutritious snack!

● **Tortillas can be warmed on an ungreased griddle or pan. For microwave warming, wrap tortillas in waxed paper and heat for a few seconds. Place on plate and cover to keep warm.**

Flour Tortillas

Tortillas are the "bread" of Mexican people. Tortillas can be fixed in a variety of ways and eaten alone they make a pleasing snack. The large, almost transluscent tortillas seen in Mexico and some Mexican households in the Southwest are evidence of the rich cultural influences carried over through the years. But, since most of us do not have the large stoves used for large tortillas, a smaller version is used. For this you will need a griddle, a willingness to learn, and perhaps a helper!

4 cups FLOUR
1½ tsp. SALT

½ cup SHORTENING
1¼ cups WARM WATER

In a mixing bowl, mix flour and salt. Cut shortening into flour and add small amounts of water while mixing. Form into a dough, knead thoroughly. Dough should be smooth and elastic. Form 18 dough balls. Sprinkle dough with flour to keep from sticking. Keep dough covered while making tortillas.

Heat griddle, but do not grease. Take a dough ball and make a circle using your hands. Using your fingers make small indentations all around the circle. With a rolling pin, flatten dough to make a 12-inch circle. Take to griddle and cook. Leave on griddle until bubbles form. Turn and cook other side. Turn only once. Place hot tortillas in a bowl or plate and cover air tight. Keep in a cool, dry place. (Makes 18 tortillas)

Store tortillas in a plastic bag or covered container.

Panecitos de Queso (Cheese Biscuits)

2 cups FLOUR
3 tsp. BAKING POWDER
2/3 tsp. SALT
4 Tbsp. chilled SHORTENING
2/3 cup grated CHEDDAR CHEESE
2/3 cup EVAPORATED MILK + 2 Tbsp. MILK

Mix flour, baking powder and salt. Add shortening in small amounts and blend in flour mixture. Sprinkle in cheese and mix. Add milk a little at a time, mixing briskly after each addition. If needed, add 2 tablespoons milk to form dough. Make a soft dough. Knead until dough holds together.

Preheat oven to 450 F. Lightly grease a baking sheet, then separate dough into 14 drop biscuits. Bake 12 to 14 minutes until golden brown. (Makes 14)

Jalapeño Corn Bread

Serve this spicy bread with soups or stews. It goes well with you favorite meat dishes!

1¼ cups YELLOW CORN MEAL
1¼ cups FLOUR
1 (level) Tbsp. BAKING POWDER
1 tsp. SALT
¼ tsp. PAPRIKA
1 tsp. SUGAR
1 well-beaten EGG
2/3 cup MILK
½ cup EVAPORATED MILK
¼ cup SHORTENING
15-oz. can CREAM-STYLE CORN
4 Tbsp. BUTTER
2 Tbsp. chopped ONION
3 JALAPEÑO CHILES, chopped or diced
4-oz. can chopped GREEN CHILES
3 Tbsp. chopped PIMIENTO
1 cup shredded CHEDDAR CHEESE

Mix corn meal, flour, baking powder, salt, sugar and paprika in a large mixing bowl. Combine egg, milk, shortening and corn. Add to dry ingredients.

In a saucepan, melt butter and saute onions, chiles and pimientos until onions are tender. Add this to rest of mixture. Mix well, but don't over-mix. Add cheese and blend in.

Butter an 8-inch square pan and pour mixture in. Heat oven to 400 F and bake for 35 minutes or until knife comes clean from center of corn bread.

When cooled, cut into pieces.

Pan Dulce (Mexican Sweet Rolls)

Dough

1¾ cup FLOUR
½ pkg. active dry YEAST
¼ tsp. ground ANISE SEED
⅛ tsp. ground CINNAMON
½ cup MILK
2 Tbsp. light BROWN SUGAR
1 Tbsp. granulated SUGAR
2 Tbsp. SHORTENING
½ tsp. SALT
1 Tbsp. CORN SYRUP
1 well-beaten EGG

In a bowl, combine 1 cup flour, yeast, anise and cinnamon. Heat milk in a saucepan, add sugars and melt shortening. Stir constantly over medium heat until shortening melts evenly. Add salt, mix until sugar is dissolved completely.

Combine milk mixture with yeast-flour mixture, plus ¾ cup flour. Add corn syrup and egg and blend well. Mix until stiff.

Take dough into hands and form into a ball. On a lightly-floured board, knead for 10 minutes until smooth and elastic. Place in a greased bowl. Cover and let sit for 1 hour, 15 minutes. Dough should be turned once. Slight pressure should leave dent in dough.

Filling

1/3 cup FLOUR
¼ cup BROWN SUGAR
1 Tbsp. granulated SUGAR
⅛ cup BUTTER
1 EGG YOLK
⅛ tsp. VANILLA
dash CINNAMON

In a mixing bowl, cream together flour, sugars and butter with a baking spoon. Add egg yolk, vanilla and cinnamon.

When dough is ready to use, knead lightly in your hands, then form 8 dough balls. Preheat oven to 375 F. Lightly grease a large baking sheet. On a lightly-floured board, flatten out dough balls to make 6-inch circles. With a spoon, spread yolk mixture over circle, then roll bottom edge of circle over (like a burrito). Make a long, deep slit over dough with a sharp knife and press down lightly. Place on baking sheet, cover and let sit for 20-30 minutes to let rise a bit more.

Bake for 15 minutes until golden brown. (Makes 8 rolls)

Mexican Corn Bread

1½ cups yellow CORN MEAL
¾ cup FLOUR
1 tsp. SALT
2½ tsp. BAKING POWDER
pinch SUGAR
¼ tsp. GARLIC POWDER
2 Tbsp. CHILI POWDER
2 EGGS
1¼ cups MILK
¼ cup melted SHORTENING
2 Tbsp. BUTTER
¼ cup diced ONION
1 cup cream-style CORN
2/3 cup shredded CHEESE (longhorn or cheddar)

In a mixing bowl, combine first seven ingredients.

In a separate bowl, loosely beat eggs, add milk and shortening. Add to dry ingredients and mix well.

In a saucepan, melt butter and saute onions until tender. Add to rest of batter.

Preheat oven to 400 F. Butter a square baking pan. Add corn and mix, then sprinkle in cheese and mix until just mixed. Place in pan, bake for 20 to 25 minutes until slightly browned. (Serves 6)

Raisin-Anise Bread

2 EGGS
½ cup SHORTENING
1½ cups BROWN SUGAR
2 cups FLOUR
3 tsp. BAKING POWDER
½ tsp. SALT
1 tsp. ground ANISE
½ tsp. ground CINNAMON
1 cup RAISINS
1 Tbsp. HONEY

Beat eggs until creamy. Cream shortening, add sugar, then mix in eggs.

Combine dry ingredients, then blend in egg mixture. Add raisins and honey. Form an elastic dough and knead well.

Preheat oven to 375 F. Butter a loaf pan. Bake for 1 hour, 15 minutes, until bread is golden brown. (Makes one pound loaf)

Mexican Corn Muffins

Mexican corn muffins go great with soups and stews and complement dinner entrees. They are also good with milk or coffee.

1 cup CORN MEAL
1 cup FLOUR
¾ Tbsp. BAKING POWDER
1 tsp. SALT
1 beaten EGG
1 cup MILK
pinch SUGAR
6-oz. can CREAMED CORN
¼ cup chopped ONION
½ cup chopped CHILES
2 Tbsp. PIMIENTOS
¼ cup BUTTER
¾ cup shredded CHEDDAR CHEESE

Combine dry ingredients and mix in large bowl. Mix beaten eggs and milk, then add sugar, add to flour mixture. Stir, then add corn. Mix.

In a saucepan, saute onions, chiles, pimientos in butter for 5 to 8 minutes. Cook until onion is tender. Add this to large bowl of flour, egg-milk mixture and stir.

Add cheese to this and mix until just mixed. Pour into two well-greased muffin or cup-cake tins. Bake in oven for 20 minutes at 400 F or until golden brown. (Makes 24 small muffins) Excellent for dipping in soup!

Aperitivos/Appetizers

Mini-Tostadas

These mini-tostadas make hearty appetizers when served with salsa.

15-oz. can REFRIED BEANS, heated
24 mini CORN TORTILLAS, pre-fried

Place beans on mini tortillas and heat in oven for a few minutes. Garnish with thinly sliced avocado, shredded cheddar cheese, sour cream mixed with chives, diced hard-boiled egg, sliced green chiles, sliced pimientos, ground beef, diced onions or salsa.

Mini-Chimichangas

Mini-chimichangas make excellent appetizers! They can be filled with any filling! Fruit chimichangas make a delicious snack or dessert. To make mini-chimis, take the smallest flour tortillas and cut them in fourths. Add one to two teaspoons filling and roll up as you would a regular size chimichanga. Deep fry to a golden brown.

Mexican Deviled Eggs

Spicy deviled eggs make a basic "appetizing" appetizer!

4 hard-boiled EGGS, cut lengthwise
4 to 5 Tbsp. MAYONNAISE
½ tsp. DRY YELLOW MUSTARD
¼ tsp. SALT
½ tsp. PAPRIKA
dash GARLIC POWDER
2 Tbsp. creamed AVOCADOS
1 Tbsp. LEMON JUICE
2 Tbsp. diced GREEN OLIVES

Mash egg yolks thoroughly. Mix mayonnaise and dry mustard and combine with yolks. Add rest of ingredients and chill for 2 minutes, then fill egg whites with yolk mixture. Sprinkle with grated cheese if desired. (Serves 4)

Quick Fried Cheese Tortillas

8-oz. can TOMATO SAUCE
6-oz. can TOMATO PASTE
¼ cup WATER
1 tsp. OREGANO
½ tsp. GARLIC SALT
½ tsp. GROUND PEPPER
BUTTER (or oil) for frying
12 FLOUR TORTILLAS
1 to 2 cups LONGHORN CHEESE
1 JALAPEÑO CHILE, cut in thin strips

In a saucepan, blend in tomato sauce and paste, add water and seasonings. Cook until thick and bubbly. Simmer covered for 10 minutes.

In a skillet, heat butter (or oil) enough to fry a flour tortilla. Place a tortilla in the skillet, then cover with the sauce and sprinkle with some cheese. As cheese melts, place another tortilla on top and butter. Turn over to fry. When both sides of tortillas are crispy brown, remove from heat, place on a plate and repeat until all tortillas and sauces are used.

Take all 6 tortilla snacks and place on a large baking sheet. Heat oven to 350 F. Sprinkle with cheese and bake until cheese melts. Top with jalapeno slices and serve. (Serves 6)

Nachos Picantes (Hot Tortilla Chips)

1 dozen CORN TORTILLAS
OIL for frying
1 cup shredded CHEESE
2 Tbsp. MILK
2 JALAPEÑO CHILES, finely diced

Take corn tortillas and cut them into fourths. Fry until golden brown, drain.

In a saucepan, melt cheese, stir in milk and mix until smooth. Add diced chiles, blend well.

Place nachos in serving bowl and pour chili/cheese sauce over them. Sprinkle with salt and pepper as desired.

Cheese Crisp #1

Cheese crisps are the perfect appetizer, so appealing but not that filling!

2 FLOUR TORTILLAS, 14-inch
BUTTER
1 cup shredded CHEDDAR CHEESE
SALSA (homemade or store bought)

Pre-heat oven to 350 F. Take pizza pan or large baking sheet and place tortillas. Butter tortillas evenly. Sprinkle with cheese and bake in oven until cheese melts and tortillas are crispy brown.
Serve cheese crisp with salsa at hand.

Cheese Crisp #2

4 CORN TORTILLAS
OIL for cooking tortillas
¾ cup grated LONGHORN CHEESE
diced, cooked GREEN CHILES
diced ONION (optional)

In a skillet, heat 3 to 4 tablespoons oil and place one corn tortilla in the hot oil. Add grated cheese evenly over tortilla, then add green chiles and onion if desired. Place another corn tortilla over cheese and chiles and cover for a few minutes. Then, turn to cook other side. Cook until cheese melts completely and tortillas turn a light golden brown. Repeat with last two tortillas. (Serves 2)

Spicy Cheese Crisp

1 large FLOUR TORTILLA
BUTTER for spreading
½ cup shredded CHEESE
2 JALAPEÑO CHILES, sliced thinly

Pre-heat oven to 350 F. Spread tortilla with butter evenly, then sprinkle with cheese. Place on baking sheet and bake until cheese melts. Add slices of jalapeno, then return to oven for a few minutes. Serve.

Spicy Jicama Sticks

Jicama (he-cah-mah) is a sweet, crisp, vegetable which resembles a potato-colored turnip. It has the taste of a water chestnut and is used by Mexican cooks as potatoes are used. Use jicama raw in place of tortilla chips. It goes great with guacamole! Alone, jicama can be sprinkled with sugar, salt, any seasoning!

1 medium-sized JICAMA
CHILI POWDER

Wash jicama thoroughly and peel. Slice into sticks and rinse in cold water, drain. Sprinkle with chili powder. Serve as part of relish tray with cheese sticks and your favorite appetizers.

Papas en Escabeche (Pickled Potatoes)

2 medium sized POTATOES, diced
4 Tbsp. WHITE VINEGAR
2 slices of ONION, sliced in pieces
2 sliced JALAPEÑOS
SALT and coarsely-ground PEPPER to taste

Boil diced potatoes until tender firm. Rinse in cold water. In a bowl, add vinegar, onion and jalapeños. Then mix in cooled potatoes. Season with salt and pepper.

Cover and refrigerate. Serve chilled the next day. Makes one bowl of papas en escabeche!

Nachos (Tortilla Chips)

Nachos serve as appetizers or snacks. Use either mini-tostadas or regular tortilla chips. You can also fry your own tortilla chips!

Take 1 dozen corn tortillas. Cut them into quarters or eighths. Fry them to a crispy brown and place in bowl lined with paper towels. Salt to taste.

Pre-heat oven to 350 F. In a round baking pan place tortilla chips, sprinkle cheese over them. Bake in oven until cheese melts. Serve with salsa, refried beans or guacamole.

Botanas/Dips

Tortilla Bean Dip

1 Tbsp. SALAD OIL
16-oz. can REFRIED BEANS
½ small ONION, diced
SALT/PEPPER to taste
2/3 cup SALSA*
1 cup crushed TORTILLA CHIPS (or nachos)
2/3 cup JACK CHEESE

In a sauce pan, heat oil and cook refried beans (mix in small amount of water). Heat to a bubbly boil, reduce heat. Add onions, seasonings and salsa*. Mix in well.

Add 1 cup crushed tortilla chips or nachos. Place dip in a casserole dish and top with jack cheese. Bake at 400 F until cheese melts. (Makes 3½ cups of dip)

*Salsa: Use store-bought salsa or use one of the salsas from this recipe book: Zesty-Quick Salsa, Salsa Picante or Salsa Rica.

Guacamole Paste

Guacamole paste makes a great dip! Spread over miniature nachos or tortilla chips.

1 large ripe AVOCADO
1 Tbsp. SOUR CREAM
2 Tbsp. minced ONION
1 fresh TOMATO, chopped
juice from ½ LIME
1 Tbsp. LEMON JUICE
¼ cup BLACK OLIVES (garnish)

In a mixing bowl, mash avocado thoroughly. Add sour cream and minced onion. Then mix in rest of ingredients. Serve in a dip bowl and sprinkle with black olives.

Garbanzo Dip

Garbanzos are often overlooked, but they can be fixed in a variety of ways. Serve as a garnish or a side dish. Here is a spicy dip!

15-oz can GARBANZOS
1 minced GARLIC CLOVE
1 tsp. OLIVE OIL
2 Tbsp. chopped PIMIENTOS
1 tsp. LEMON JUICE
SALT/PEPPER

Place ingredients in a blender and mix well. Serve in dip bowl with nachos or any chips! (Makes 1 bowl of dip)

Chile con Queso (Mild)

2 Tbsp. BUTTER
1 Tbsp. FLOUR
1 cup MILK
dash SALT/PEPPER
1 cup grated LONGHORN CHEESE
4-oz. can diced GREEN CHILES
2 Tbsp. diced PIMIENTOS

In a saucepan, melt butter, blend in flour. Add milk and heat to a boil until thick, stir constantly.

Reduce heat, add seasonings and cheese. Cook until cheese melts completely. Add chiles and pimientos. Cook until thickened. Serve hot. (Makes 1¾ cups)

Chile con Queso (Zesty)

2 Tbsp. BUTTER
1 Tbsp. FLOUR
1 cup MILK
dash SALT/PEPPER/GARLIC POWDER
1 cup grated CHEDDAR CHEESE
4-oz. can diced or sliced GREEN CHILES
1 to 2 diced JALAPEÑO CHILES

Melt butter, blend in flour. Add milk; bring to a fast boil, stirring constantly. Add seasonings, cheese and chiles. Cook over medium heat until thickened. (Makes 1¾ cups) Excellent with nachos.

Cheese Dip

A good cheese dip is always a welcome appetizer! Serve this cheese dip with miniature taco shells, lettuce and olives.

5 Tbsp. OIL
2 Tbsp. PIMIENTOS, diced
1 JALAPEÑO CHILE, diced
2 cups CHEDDAR CHEESE
¼ tsp. PEPPER
¼ tsp. SALT
½ tsp. PAPRIKA
CHIVES to garnish

Heat oil and saute pimientos and chile. Add cheese and melt. Stir in seasonings, blend well. Place in a dip bowl and whip to a creamy texture. Serve with any chips or raw vegetables!

Bean Dip with Cheese

1 Tbsp. SALAD OIL
2 Tbsp. diced ONION
15-oz. can REFRIED BEANS + small amount of water
SALT to taste
½ cup shredded CHEESE

In a saucepan, heat oil, saute onions. Add beans and a little water. Mix and mash beans. Add salt to taste. When beans come to a bubbly boil, remove from heat and place in dip bowl. Sprinkle cheese and blend into hot beans so cheese melts completely.

Jalapeño Bean Dip

1 Tbsp. SALAD OIL
15-oz. can REFRIED BEANS + small amount of water
1 Tbsp. diced ONION
SALT to taste
pinch of GARLIC SALT
½ cup shredded CHEESE
2 minced JALAPEÑO CHILES

In a saucepan, heat oil, add beans, mix with a little water. Stir in onions, salt, garlic salt. Add cheese, allow to melt. Sprinkle with chiles. Heat until beans are slightly thickened. Place in dip bowl, serve with tortilla chips. (Makes 1 bowl of dip)

Guacamole Dip

Guacamole makes a superb dip! Serve it chilled, with tortilla chips. Guacamole also makes an excellent garnish for most Mexican dishes.

2 large AVOCADOS, mashed
1 tsp. LEMON JUICE
SALT/PEPPER to taste
dash GARLIC POWDER
2 Tbsp. diced ONION
1 small TOMATO, diced
4-oz. can diced GREEN CHILES
1 Tbsp. PIMIENTOS
¼ cup shredded CHEESE

Mash avocados well, add lemon juice, salt, pepper, garlic powder, blend well. Add onions, tomato, green chiles, pimientos, mix. Place dip in blender for desired thickness. Place in bowl and chill before serving. Sprinkle with cheese. Serve with chips. (Makes 3 cups)

Meat Dip

This meat dip serves as a good appetizer to a meatless entree. It is tasty with any chips and your favorite vegetables.

1 Tbsp. OIL
1 Tbsp. diced ONION
2 cups cooked GROUND BEEF
dash OREGANO, SALT, PEPPER
⅛ tsp. GARLIC POWDER
6-oz. can TOMATO SAUCE
2 Tbsp. TOMATO PASTE
1 cup WATER

Heat oil and briefly saute onions. Add meat and seasonings. Mix well. Add tomato sauce and paste. Blend in. Then add water and cook for a few minutes for desired thickness. (Makes 1 bowl of dip)

Sopas/Soups

Albondigas (Meatball Soup)

Albondigas soup is a hearty soup which can be served as an entree.

> 1 lb. GROUND BEEF
> 3 Tbsp. diced ONION
> ¼ tsp. OREGANO
> SALT/PEPPER
> 1 BAY LEAF
> 6 cups WATER
> 4 to 5 chopped stewed TOMATOES
> ½ cup pre-cooked white RICE
> 1 cup cooked, tender-firm sliced POTATOES

Take raw meat and blend in onion. Add oregano, salt, pepper. Form 18 meat balls.

In a 2-quart cooking pot, add water, the chopped tomatoes and bay leaf. Add meat balls and cook over medium heat, covered.

When meat is fully stewed, remove bay leaf, add rice and sliced potatoes. Simmer over low heat covered until potatoes are tender. (Serves 6)

Cazuela

This delicious meat soup is often made with brisket or **Carne Seca** (see recipe).

> 1 Tbsp. OIL
> 1 Tbsp. FLOUR
> 2 to 3 GREEN ONIONS, chopped
> 3 to 4 cups WATER
> SALT/PEPPER to taste
> dash GARLIC POWDER
> 4-oz. can GREEN CHILES
> (or 2 sliced fresh green chiles)
> 1 to 1½ lbs. cooked BRISKET, shredded or sliced

In a cooking pot, heat oil and brown flour. Saute green onion, add water. Add seasonings and bring to a fast boil.

Add green chile (canned or fresh). Add meat and blend in well. If necessary, add hot water in small amounts. Cover and let simmer over reduced heat for 15 to 20 minutes. (Serves 6 to 8)

Lentil Soup #1

8 cups WATER
6 slices uncooked BACON (cut in pieces)
1 diced CARROT
1 cup LENTILS, rinsed
1 tsp. GARLIC SALT
¼ tsp. SALT
½ medium ONION, whole

In a 3-quart cooking pot, add water and bacon. After water has come to a boil, cook for 30 minutes over medium heat. Add carrots, lentils, seasonings and onion. Cover and cook for 1½ hours. Remove onion. (Makes 4 to 5 servings)

Menudo (Tripe Soup)

Menudo is a savory soup, very much a part of Mexican culture. The aroma of a large pot of menudo simmering in the kitchen fills the entire house!

Some people may be put off by the thought of eating beef tripe, the "meat" used for menudo, but it really is delicious. Uncooked beef tripe has a strong odor which is not particularly pleasing, but the outcome is truly worth it!

In Sonora, menudo is made with chili powder and a rich, zesty red soup results. Menudo in the Southwest is always garnished with chopped chives and served with hot corn tortillas!

1½ to 2 lbs. BEEF TRIPE
4 quarts cold WATER
1 clove GARLIC
2 whole small ONIONS
2 tsp. SALT
PEPPER to taste
29-oz. can HOMINY (white)
chopped CHIVES for garnish

Wash tripe thoroughly and soak in cold water overnight. Cut tripe into small bite-sized pieces. Put tripe into a large cooking pot and add water, garlic clove and onions. Add salt and pepper to taste. Cook, covered, over medium heat until tripe is tender. Add hominy and mix in well. Simmer 10 minutes. Remove garlic clove and onions. Serve with chopped chives. Makes a potful! (Serves 8-10)

Sopa de Conchitas (Macaroni Soup)

Conchitas means shells. This macaroni soup is often a lunchtime dish in our house. With cheese it becomes a tasty macaroni and cheese dish. The secret to this savory soup is the meat stock. Always use meat stock instead of water or bouillon cubes!

1 Tbsp. salad or olive OIL
8 oz. SHELL MACARONI
1 Tbsp. diced ONION
½ cup diced GREEN PEPPER
4 large, chopped, stewed TOMATOES
SALT/PEPPER to taste
dash GARLIC SALT
3 cups MEAT STOCK (beef or chicken)

In a skillet or cooking pot, heat oil and lightly brown macaroni. Add onions and green peppers, saute until green peppers are tender firm. Add chopped tomatoes and seasonings. Add meat stock plus hot water if necessary for adequate soup stock. Add ½ cup to 1 cup, depending on how much soup stock you want. If your meat stock is frozen, leave frozen and while macaroni is cooking, check and blend in stock as it melts. Cover and cook over reduced heat for 45 minutes until macaroni is fully cooked and green peppers are tender. (Serves 6)

Lentil Soup #2

2 cups uncooked, washed LENTILS
3 quarts cold WATER
½ lb. uncooked BACON, separated slices, cut into halves
1 small ONION, cut in rings
1 tsp. OLIVE OIL
2 tsp. SALT
1 GARLIC CLOVE (minced)
1 BAY LEAF

Wash lentils and soak in cold water for an hour. In a cooking pot, combine lentils, water, bacon, onion, olive oil and salt. Bring to a boil. Add garlic clove and bay leaf. Cover, simmer over reduced heat for 4 to 5 minutes until bacon is fully cooked. Remove bay leaf, season to taste and serve hot. (Serves 6)

For *zest*, add tabasco sauce of salsa to lentil soup!

Caldo de Queso (Cheese Soup)

Serve this zesty soup with hot corn tortillas, flour tortillas, hard rolls, bread sticks or sprinkle with croutons.

3 Tbsp. OIL
3 Tbsp. FLOUR
⅛ sm. ONION, diced
6 cups WATER
1 tsp. SALT
3 dashes of PEPPER
¼ tsp. GARLIC POWDER
3 CHILES (Anaheim) diced
1 cup LONGHORN CHEESE, grated
3 med.-sized POTATOES, diced

In a 2-quart cooking pot, add oil and heat. Brown flour, then add diced onions. Cook for a few minutes. Add 6 cups of water to this mixture. Stir constantly. Let boil and simmer for 10 minutes. Add salt, pepper, garlic powder and diced chiles. Set aside covered.

Add 1 cup of cheese to the pot. Then add diced potatoes and return to medium heat. Cook until potatoes are tender. Cheese must be completely melted. Sprinkle with pepper and serve. Makes 4 servings.

Sopa de Fideo (Pasta Soup)

½ lb. uncooked BEEF (or chicken) sliced or diced
8 oz. uncooked FIDEO
6-oz. can TOMATO SAUCE
½ tsp. ground THYME (coarse)
SALT/PEPPER to taste
1 BAY LEAF
2 Tbsp. ONIONS chopped (optional)

Cook meat in 2½ quarts or so water, covered, until meat is tender and well cooked. Chop meat to desired pieces. Drain meat, but save all the stock.

Break fideo into pieces and lightly brown in a large skillet or cooking pot, using salad oil or olive oil for browning. Add 5 cups of meat stock, and tomato sauce. Stir and mix well. Save any remaining stock for later use. Add thyme, salt, pepper, and onions, if desired.

Add bay leaf and cook over low heat, covered, until fideo is tender. Remove bay leaf. (Serves 6)

Chili Bean Soup

Chili beans can be made with pot beans or kidney beans. Served with crackers, this soup is a favorite. Here is a recipe for spicy chili bean soup!

1/3 cup FLOUR
OIL to brown flour
3¼ Tbsp. CHILI POWDER
3 cups WATER
1 tsp. SALT
¼ tsp. PEPPER
¼ tsp. GARLIC POWDER
½ small ONION, diced
15-oz. can KIDNEY BEANS (drained)

In a skillet, add enough oil to brown flour and make a basic gravy. To 3 cups of water, dissolve chili powder, then add to skillet and mix well. Add seasonings and onions. Cover, cook briefly over low heat, then add kidney beans, mix. Cover, simmer 20 minutes. (Serves 4-6)

Chili With Pot Beans

To your cooked pot beans, add 4 Tbsp. chili powder, onion and 1 cup ground beef for meaty chili beans.

Sopa de Verdolagas (Purslane Soup)

To make this soup, use only the leaves of the verdolagas. Choose the most tender and youngest weeds.

3 cups CHICKEN BROTH (fresh or frozen thawed)
½ small ONION, cut in thin rings
3 to 4 stewed TOMATOES, chopped
1 tsp. fresh dried crushed CILANTRO
⅛ tsp. GARLIC SALT
SALT to taste
1 cup cooked VERDOLAGAS, chopped

In a quart cooking pot, heat chicken broth, add onion, tomatoes and cilantro. Heat to a slow boil, reduce heat, add garlic salt and salt to taste. Simmer 5 minutes, covered. Add verdolagas, then serve. (Serves 4-5)

Posole

Posole is a bean, meat and hominy soup. In Sonora, posole has a chili soup base. Typically, posole is made with pork, but beef can also be used.

3 quarts WATER
2 cups PINTO BEANS
1½ lbs. CHUCK BEEF (or 1½ lbs. pork)
    cut in bite-sized pieces
1 small ONION sliced in thin rings
1 GARLIC CLOVE, minced
1 BAY LEAF
1 Tbsp. SALT
⅛ tsp. OREGANO
15-oz. can WHITE HOMINY, drained

Bring water to a fast boil. Add all ingredients EXCEPT hominy. Cook until beans and meat are tender (over medium heat) about 1 hour 25 minutes, covered. Add hot water in small amounts as needed during cooking. Remove bay leaf. During last 10 minutes of cooking, add hominy. Mix well. (Serves 6-8)

Gazpacho

Typically, gazpacho is a cold soup served with salsa. It can contain corn or squash or include orange slices! Here is one version:

15-oz. can drained GARBANZO BEANS
1 large CUCUMBER, peeled, sliced
2 large TOMATOES, peeled, chopped in small pieces
1 small GREEN PEPPER, seeded, sliced
3 cups boiling WATER
1 tsp. SALT
½ tsp. PEPPER
1 Tbsp. TABASCO SAUCE (or hot sauce)
1 small LIME, sliced thinly

In a serving bowl, combine garbanzos, cucumber slices, chopped tomatoes and green peppers.

To boiling water, add salt, pepper and tabasco sauce or hot salsa. Blend thoroughly. Pour mixture into serving bowl, add sliced lime, let stand 5 minutes. Serve. (Serves 4-5)

Caldo Ranchero (Ranch Soup)

This soup is quite a hefty soup which could also be called a stew. "Cocido" is another name for stew in Spanish, but caldo ranchero received its title as a soup because of the variety of ingredients that can go in it! It can be soup or stew depending on how you make it!

Caldo Ranchero means ranch style soup. It goes well with corn bread or any hard roll. It can also be served with rolled, plain tacos filled with cheese or your favorite filling.

> 2 lbs. CHUCK ROAST (or brisket or any beef)
> 3 quarts WATER
> 5 Tbsp. OIL
> 5 Tbsp. FLOUR
> 1 small ONION, coarsely chopped
> 1 whole GARLIC CLOVE
> 4 cooked CORN ON THE COB, divided into ¼'s
> 4 chopped TOMATOES
> 2 tsp. SALT
> 1/3 tsp. PEPPER
> 1 BAY LEAF
> 1 small cooked CAULIFLOWER,
>   divided into small sprigs

Chop meat into bite-size pieces and cook in lightly-salted water (3 quarts) until meat is tender and well cooked. Cook in covered cooking pot, stirring occasionally. Skim off fat and take out 2 cups of soup stock, set aside.

In a saucepan, heat oil and brown the flour. Saute onions, then add 2 cups of soup stock and mix thoroughly.

In a Dutch oven, add meat and stock plus gravy mixture. Blend well. Stir in garlic clove, corn, tomatoes, cauliflower, seasonings and bay leaf. Add up to 3 cups more water if needed to keep adequate soup stock.

Over medium heat, cook, covered, for 45 minutes, stirring occasionally. Remove bay leaf. Serve with avocado salad. (Serves 6-8)

● **Mexican food should be served piping hot to insure the flavor.**

Ensaladas/Salads

Topopo Salad

Salads weren't very common in Mexico. Topopo salad is a "contemporary" salad. It is popular both in Mexico and the Southwest. Here is a family favorite with its own **Spicy Sour Cream Dressing.**

LETTUCE
diced, fresh TOMATOES
strips of CHICKEN, HAM
AVOCADO strips
CHEDDAR CHEESE strips
sliced BLACK OLIVES

Topopo salad should be served individually, topped with your favorite dressing.

Line salad bowls with lettuce, use bigger leaves for this. Shred lettuce and fill bowls 2/3 full. Add strips of chicken and ham together, forming a mound. Sprinkle meats with coarsely-ground black pepper. Take avocado strips and place around meats. Sprinkle with diced tomatoes and cheddar cheese. Season lightly with salt/pepper.

Serve with **Spicy Sour Cream Dressing.**

Spicy Sour Cream Dressing

1 cup SOUR CREAM
2 Tbsp. LEMON JUICE
2 Tbsp. minced PIMIENTOS
¼ tsp. SALT
⅛ tsp. PAPRIKA
dash GARLIC POWDER
2 drops TABASCO SAUCE

In a bowl, add sour cream and mix in rest of ingredients. Use blender for desired thickness. Chill before serving. (Makes 1 cup)

Ensalada de Papa y Jicama
(Potato and Jicama Salad)

2 cups cooked, diced POTATOES
2 cups cooked JICAMA
½ cup diced GREEN PEPPER
¾ cup MAYONNAISE
2 Tbsp. SOUR CREAM
2 Tbsp. RED WINE (or sherry)
1½ tsp. SALT
¼ tsp. PEPPER
⅛ tsp. OREGANO
pinch SUGAR
1 Tbsp. LEMON JUICE
½ cup diced RED ONION

In a large mixing bowl, combine potatoes and jicama. Add green pepper. In a separate bowl, mix mayonnaise, sour cream and red wine. Add all seasonings and sugar. Add lemon juice and diced onion, blend well.

Combine mayonnaise mixture with potatoes and jicama. Blend thoroughly. Add diced hard-boiled eggs if desired. Cover, chill. (Serves 8-10)

Corn Salad

12-oz. can WHOLE KERNEL CORN, drained
½ medium RED ONION, chopped
1 fresh TOMATO, chopped
½ cup diced GREEN PEPPER
½ cup chopped GREEN ONION
1 Tbsp. chopped PARSLEY
SALT/PEPPER to taste
¼ cup CILANTRO, crushed leaves
4 Tbsp. WHITE VINEGAR

In a bowl, mix all ingredients and chill for 30 minutes. Garnish with avocado slices. (Serves 4)

Taco Salad

Great for parties! It's inexpensive to make and very satisfying.

**1 bag of any name brand *plain* TORTILLA CHIPS,
    crushed or whole
fresh TOMATOES, chopped
chopped GREEN PEPPER
3 chopped hard-boiled EGGS
½ lb. well-cooked, lightly-seasoned GROUND BEEF,
    chopped
1 cup diced CHEDDAR CHEESE
½ cup Monterey JACK CHEESE, grated
1 large CUCUMBER, sliced**

Mix all the ingredients in a large salad bowl. Season with salt/pepper to taste.

The **Avocado Sauce** in the **Salsa/Sauces** section of the book is quite good with this salad. Just mix in blender to make a dressing.

Sprinkle with seasoned croutons, if desired!

Chile Verde (Green Chile) Salad

Chile verde is delicious raw!

**LETTUCE
3 large uncooked ANAHEIM CHILES, sliced
1 medium CUCUMBER, sliced
4 fresh TOMATOES, chopped
1/3 cup grated CARROTS**

In individual salad bowls, add lettuce, thinly-sliced cucumbers, tomatoes and garnish with carrots. Use oil-and-vinegar dressing. (Makes 4 salads)

Raw chile verde can be used for many dishes. It can be sauted in eggs, stir-fried in meat dishes and used as garnish. Use your favorite vegetables and chile for a new taste!

Avocado Salad

LETTUCE
2 chopped, hard-boiled EGGS
3 AVOCADOS, thinly sliced
½ cup sliced GREEN OLIVES
small salad ONION, sliced in thin rings
PAPRIKA
SALT/PEPPER to taste
OIL-AND-VINEGAR DRESSING

Line a salad bowl with the bigger leaves of the lettuce, then chop the rest. Place thinly-sliced avocado and olives on salad. Sprinkle with chopped egg and add onions. Sprinkle with paprika, salt/pepper to taste. Use a basic oil-and-vinegar dressing. (Serves 6)

Try *olive oil* and vinegar for a change!

Ensalada de Papa (Potato Salad)

3 cups cooked POTATOES, diced (chilled)
½ cup MAYONNAISE
¼ cup SOUR CREAM
1 Tbsp. LEMON JUICE
2 Tbsp. RED WINE VINEGAR
½ tsp. SALT
¼ tsp. coarsely ground PEPPER
1½ cups diced GREEN PEPPER
½ cup diced ONION
2 JALAPEÑO CHILES, thinly sliced
6 strips crisp BACON, chilled, crushed

Chill diced potatoes in salad bowl. In a bowl, mix mayonnaise and sour cream. Add lemon juice and vinegar. Blend well. Season with salt, pepper, add green pepper and onion. Mix in diced potatoes and chiles. Mix thoroughly. Garnish with bacon. Chill until ready to serve. (Serves 5)

Platos de Entrada/ Side Dishes

Frijoles (Beans)

Pot beans are a food basic in most Mexican households. Pinto beans, the beans most used, can be prepared enteros (whole), moledos (mashed/creamed), or re-fritos (refried). Beans make a basic side dish for any Mexican meal, with cheese or salsa as garnish. Creamed or mashed, beans are used for tostadas, tacos, burros and dips.

2 cups PINTO BEANS*
1 Tbsp. SALT
WATER for cooking

Clean beans, wash in cold water. In a cooking pot, bring 1 1/3 quarts of water to a boil. Add salt. Add beans, reduce heat to medium and cover. Cook beans until they are tender and brownish pink in color, 1 hour, 25 minutes.

*Pot beans can be stored right in the cooking pot with a lid for up to a week in a refrigerator.

Frijoles con Chorizo (Beans and Sausage)

2 tsp. SALAD OIL
2 cups cooked PINTO BEANS
⅛ tsp. GARLIC SALT
SALT to taste
1 cup cooked, drained CHORIZO
    (store-bought or homemade)
1/3 cup chopped ONION
¼ cup dried, crushed CILANTRO
CHEDDAR CHEESE to garnish

In a skillet, heat oil, add cooked pinto beans and mash with a potato masher. Cook beans for 2 minutes, then sprinkle with garlic salt and salt. Add cooked and well-drained chorizo. Blend well. Add onion and cilantro. Cover, let simmer over low heat for 10 to 15 minutes. Stir frequently. Serve as a side dish. Garnish with shredded cheese or salsa. (Serves 4 to 5)

Frijoles Moledos y Fritos (Refried Beans)

2 cups cooked PINTO BEANS
2 tsp. OIL
1 crushed GARLIC CLOVE
1 Tbsp. chopped ONION
pinch SALT
¾ cup shredded LONGHORN CHEESE

Heat oil and add beans. Mash beans thoroughly, add a little water, the garlic clove, onion and salt. Cook beans until they are well heated. Add cheese and cook until it melts completely. Serve hot as a side dish. Makes a good dip. (Serves 4 to 6)

Spicy Pot Beans

Turn your fresh pot beans into a spicy Mexican treat!

fresh pot of cooked PINTO BEANS
3 cups SOUP STOCK (from cooked beans)
5 Tbsp. CHILI POWDER
1 tsp. SALT

Prepare 2 cups of pinto beans (see recipe for **Frijoles**). Add soup stock (use hot water to make the difference if you don't have 3 cups), chili powder and salt. Blend in well and bring to a boil. (Makes 1 pot of **Spicy Pot Beans**)

Chorizo y Frijoles (Sausage and Beans)

2 cups PINTO BEANS
1 1/3 quarts WATER
1 Tbsp. SALT
¼ lb. CHORIZO
1 Tbsp. diced ONION

Cook pinto beans as described in **Frijoles** recipe.
In a skillet or fry pan, cook chorizo and drain well. Using the same skillet add beans, drained, and mash with potato masher. Cream beans well. Add drained chorizo and blend in well. Then add diced onion. Cook beans over medium heat until bubbly hot. Garnish with shredded cheese as desired. (Serves 6)

Arroz (Rice)

Rice is a favorite and basic side dish which complements most Mexican food.

3 Tbsp. OIL (salad oil or olive oil)
½ lb. long-grain white RICE
¼ medium ONION, diced
4 to 5 cups CHICKEN STOCK*
½ tsp. PEPPER
1 Tbsp. SALT
6-oz. can TOMATO SAUCE
¾ cup WATER

Heat oil in skillet, add rice and cook until brown, stirring constantly over medium heat. Add diced onion and cook until onion is tender. Add stock and stir well. Then add pepper, salt, tomato sauce and water. Cook over medium heat, covered, for 45-50 minutes. Rice should be tender; stir often to keep from sticking. (Makes 6-8 servings)

*Arroz (rice) tastes best when meat stock is used as opposed to bouillon cubes which tend to be too salty. Chicken stock is favored, since it has a more subtle taste and can go with meat dishes without being inappropriate in taste. A good cook knows to save meat stock. Use milk cartons cut in half and freeze stock with a freezer-safe covering. Then, when you are ready to use your stock, you can remove the carton easily with warm water. So, next time you cook meat, think about saving the stock. Rice made with shrimp stock is also very delicious!

Arroz Sabroso

2 Tbsp. OLIVE OIL
½ cup diced GREEN PEPPERS
½ cup chopped CELERY
3 Tbsp. diced ONION
¼ tsp. GARLIC POWDER
SALT/PEPPER to taste
dash OREGANO
3½ cups cooked BROWN RICE
3 TOMATOES, chopped

In a skillet, heat oil and saute peppers, celery and onions until all are tender. Add spices, stir well over medium heat! Add rice and mix then add chopped tomatoes. Reduce heat to low, cover for 5 minutes. (Serves 6)

Arroz con Chorizo (Rice and Sausage)

¼ lb. CHORIZO
2 Tbsp. OLIVE OIL
1 cup long grain RICE
2 cups MEAT BROTH (preferably chicken)
SALT to taste
¼ tsp. PEPPER
¼ tsp. OREGANO
1/3 cup chopped GREEN ONIONS
½ cup cooked PEAS, drained
2 small TOMATOES, chopped

In a fry pan, take chorizo and cook it. Drain and set aside in a warmer. In a skillet, heat oil and brown the rice. Add meat broth slowly, then blend in seasonings. Cook for a few minutes. Then add chorizo. Cook covered for 40 minutes until rice is tender. Add green onions, peas and tomatoes. Stir, cover and simmer 5 minutes. Serve hot (Makes 4 servings)

Arroz con Pimientos

1 Tbsp. OLIVE OIL
1 cup uncooked BROWN RICE
½ GARLIC CLOVE, minced
½ small ONION, chopped
3 cups MEAT STOCK (or bouillon cubes)
2/3 cup CORN (frozen, canned or fresh-cooked)
½ cup PIMIENTOS, cut in strips
½ cup grated CHEESE
2 Tbsp. soft BREAD CRUMBS

In a skillet, heat olive oil and brown rice. Add garlic clove and chopped onion. Saute until onion is tender. Add chicken stock or beef stock. Add corn. Cook until rice is fully cooked, covered, stirring occasionally. Add pimientos and cheese, mix in. Add bread crumbs, mix, simmer for 15 minutes, covered. (Serves 6)

Spanish Rice

1 Tbsp. OLIVE OIL
2 cups cooked white RICE
large pinch SAFFRON
SALT to taste
dash CAYENNE PEPPER
dash PAPRIKA
¼ cup diced GREEN PEPPER
¼ cup diced PIMIENTO
½ cup CHICKEN STOCK (or beef stock)

In a skillet, heat olive oil and saute onion. Add rice and stir fry for 1 to 2 minutes. Add saffron, salt, pepper and paprika. Blend in green pepper and pimiento. Add meat stock and ½ cup water and cook, covered, until green pepper is tender. (Serves 4 or 5)

Mexican Rice

½ lb. long-grain RICE
3 Tbsp. SHORTENING
½ small ONION, chopped
1 GARLIC CLOVE, minced
4 to 5 cups CHICKEN BROTH (fresh or canned)
½ cup frozen, thawed PEAS
3 to 4 stewed TOMATOES, chopped
1 small GREEN PEPPER, diced
1 tsp. crushed CILANTRO, fresh dried
½ tsp. SALT

Place rice in hot water and soak for 15 minutes. Work rice through with your fingers when the water is warm enough to handle. Rinse in cold water and repeat until water from rice comes clear. Spread rice over waxed paper to dry out evenly. While rice is drying, chop onions, prepare broth, thaw peas, chop tomatoes and dice peppers.

When rice is dry, heat shortening in a skillet and fry rice over medium heat. Add onion and cook until fairly softened. Add minced garlic clove and chicken broth. Cook to a boil, reduce heat to simmer. Add cilantro and salt. Blend in diced pepper and chopped tomatoes. Cover and cook for 40 minutes stirring frequently to from sticking. Add peas and cook for an additional 5 minutes. (Serves 6 to 8)

Chilaquilas (Chilaquilles)

Chilaquilas are a sort of "tortilla-mash" made of corn tortillas. They serve well as a side dish, especially tasty with meat entrees.

6 to 8 CORN TORTILLAS, cut into eighths
3 Tbsp. OIL
3 Tbsp. FLOUR
2 cups WATER
6 Tbsp. CHILI POWDER
SALT/PEPPER to taste
dash GARLIC POWDER
½ small ONION, diced
½ cup sliced GREEN OLIVES
1 cup grated LONGHORN CHEESE

Cut corn tortillas into eighths in triangles. Make a basic chili sauce by heating oil and browning flour. Dissolve chili powder in water and set aside. Add seasonings to browned flour and stir well over medium heat.

In a skillet, saute onions in a bit of oil. Add tortilla pieces to sauteed onions and soften. Add green olives and mix. Then add chili sauce to this mixture, stirring thoroughly. Cook for 5 minutes over medium heat. Add cheese, stir and leave covered over low heat. Serve when cheese is melted. (Makes 4-6 servings)

Mexican Skillet Potatoes

3 large BAKING POTATOES, peeled, diced
3 to 4 Tbsp. BACON FAT
    (or safflower or salad oil)
½ small ONION, cut in rings
1 small GREEN PEPPER, diced
SALT
¼ tsp. coarsely ground PEPPER
4 crushed CILANTRO leaves

Rinse diced potatoes thoroughly. Heat oil in skillet and cook potatoes, covered, over medium heat until tender firm. Add onion, green pepper and salt. Cover and cook until green pepper is tender. Season with pepper and cilantro. Simmer 10 minutes. Serve hot. (Serves 4 to 5)

Spicy Garbanzos

3 Tbsp. FLOUR
3 Tbsp. OIL
2 Tbsp. diced PIMIENTO
2 Tbsp. diced ONION
2 chopped STEWED TOMATOES
2 Tbsp. chopped, cooked GREEN CHILES
1 cup WATER
15-oz. can GARBANZO BEANS, drained
SALT/PEPPER to taste
pinch GARLIC SALT

In a skillet, brown flour in oil. Add onion and pimiento, saute until onion is tender. Add tomatoes and chiles to make a thickish gravy mixture. Add water and garbanzos, blend well, then add seasonings. Simmer 10 minutes, covered, over low heat. Stir occasionally. Remove from heat, simmer 5 minutes. (4 to 6 servings)

Mexican Creamed Spinach

4 Tbsp. salad OIL
4 Tbsp. FLOUR
16-oz. can SPINACH
4 diced TOMATOES
3 Tbsp. diced ONION
¼ tsp. PEPPER
½ tsp. SALT
⅛ tsp. GARLIC POWDER

In a skillet, heat oil and brown flour. Saute onions until tender, then add tomatoes. Cook 1 minute. Add drained spinach and seasonings, mix well. Cover, let simmer over low heat for 15 minutes, stirring occasionally. Serve hot. Sprinkle with diced pimientos if desired. (Serves 4)

Mexican Green Beans

2 Tbsp. OIL
2 Tbsp. FLOUR
3 Tbsp. CHILI POWDER
¾ cup WATER
SALT to taste
¼ tsp. GARLIC SALT

16-oz. can GREEN BEANS, drained
½ cup grated CHEESE

In a saucepan, heat oil and brown the flour. Dissolve chili powder in water, then add to browned flour. Add seasonings, mix in green beans. Add cheese and cover, simmering until cheese melts completely. Keep covered until ready to serve. (Serves 4)

Guacamole

Guacamole is a complement to any Mexican dish and it also makes a great dip! Serve with tortilla chips or with any Mexican entree. Serve with **Enchiladas** for an added taste sensation.

2 large AVOCADOS, mashed
1 tsp. LEMON JUICE
1 small yellow ONION, chopped
1 minced GARLIC CLOVE (or ½ tsp. garlic powder)
1 tsp. SALT
dash PEPPER
1 Tbsp. PIMIENTOS
2 Tbsp. GREEN CHILES, chopped
2 Tbsp. MAYONNAISE

Thoroughly mash avocados until creamy. Add lemon juice, mix. Then add onion and minced garlic. Add salt, pepper and pimientos. Add chiles, mix thoroughly. Add mayonnaise and whip to creamy texture.

Calabacitas con Jamón
(Squash and Ham)

3 Tbsp. SALAD OIL
1 small ONION, cut in rings
1 medium GREEN PEPPER, cut in strips
1 small PIMIENTO, cut in strips
2 large fresh TOMATOES, coarsely chopped
2 cups cooked YELLOW SQUASH
4 cups cooked HAM, cut in strips
½ tsp. SALT
¼ tsp. PEPPER
⅛ tsp. GARLIC POWDER
2 tsp. PARSLEY FLAKES

In a skillet, heat oil and saute onions. Add green peppers and pimientos and cook a few minutes. Add rest of ingredients plus seasonings, blend in well. Cover and simmer 15 minutes, until green pepper is tender. (Serves 4 to 5)

For a really tasty dish, use chicken stock! Take ½ cup or so fresh or frozen thawed chicken stock and cook covered for 20 to 25 minutes.

Calabacitas (Squash)

Kids who don't like vegetables will like squash fixed this way! Calabacitas go well with meat dishes.

2 lbs. SUMMER SQUASH, diced in bite-size pieces
1 Tbsp. vegetable OIL
2 Tbsp. diced ONION
3 STEWED TOMATOES, cut in pieces
1 cup cheddar or longhorn CHEESE, grated
8-oz. can yellow WHOLE CORN
½ tsp. SALT
PEPPER to taste

Boil diced squash until tender, 15-20 minutes, over medium heat. Drain and leave in colander. In cooking pot, add oil and saute onion and tomatoes. Add squash to this, mix well. Mix in salt and pepper to taste. Continue heating. Add grated cheese and allow to melt. Add corn, stir. Cook 1-2 minutes. Serve when cheese is fully melted. (Serves 6)

For added zest, mix in a 4-oz. can of diced, cooked green chiles.

Calabacitas con Chile (Zucchini and Chile)

2 lbs. ZUCCHINI, diced in bite-size pieces
1 Tbsp. SALAD OIL
½ small ONION, diced
3 fresh TOMATOES, chopped
4 to 5 chopped, cooked GREEN CHILES
½ tsp. SALT, PEPPER as desired
dash GARLIC POWDER
2/3 cup shredded JACK CHEESE

Cook zucchini until tender, over medium heat. Drain. In a skillet, heat oil and saute onion. Add tomatoes, green chiles and seasonings. Blend in well. Cook for a few minutes over reduced heat. Add cheese, mix in well. Cover, heat 1 to 2 minutes. Serve when cheese is fully melted. (Serves 6)

Verdolagas (Purslane)

Verdolagas is a common "weed" in the southwest. It grows in the summer months and is best used raw or lightly cooked. To use, cut at the roots, choose only tender, young weeds that have not been exposed to pesticides. Verdolagas can also be purchased in grocery stores.

Wash well, then strip leaves from the stems of the verdolagas and stew-cook leaves until just tender. Overcooking gives verdolagas a smooth, slippery texture and a dark green color.

2 tsp. OLIVE OIL
2 tsp. FLOUR
1 cup cooked VERDOLAGAS, drained, chopped
2 Tbsp. diced ONION
4 oz. diced GREEN CHILES
2 fresh TOMATOES, chopped
shredded JACK CHEESE as garnish

In skillet, heat oil and brown flour. Add verdolagas and onion. Cook for one minute. Add green chiles and tomatoes. Blend well. Cover to simmer a few minutes. Serve with shredded jack cheese. (Serves 4)

Verdolagas con Chile y Queso

3 Tbsp. OIL
3 Tbsp. FLOUR
2 cups CHICKEN BROTH (or stock)
6 Tbsp. CHILI POWDER
1 tsp. SALT
⅛ tsp. GARLIC POWDER
1 cup VERDOLAGAS LEAVES, cooked
2/3 cup grated LONGHORN CHEESE

In a skillet, heat oil and brown flour. Dissolve chili powder in chicken broth or stock, then blend in with browned flour. Simmer, add seasonings then verdolagas and cheese. Allow cheese to melt, serve at once. (Serves 5)

Fiesta Hominy

This colorful side dish goes great with meat dishes, a novel alternative to potatoes.

3 Tbsp. FLOUR
3 Tbsp. OIL
2 Tbsp. diced ONION
½ medium GREEN PEPPER, sliced
1 medium TOMATO
29-oz. can WHITE HOMINY
2 cups WATER
SALT/PEPPER to taste
dash GARLIC POWDER

Brown flour in oil. Add diced onion and saute. Then add sliced pepper and tomato. Stir over medium heat. Add drained hominy, stir, add 2 cups water. Stir in pepper, salt and garlic powder. Simmer 10 to 15 minutes, covered, over medium heat. Stir occasionally. Leave covered until ready to serve. (Makes 6 servings)

Chile/Cheese Potatoes

4 medium BAKING POTATOES
¾ cup SOUR CREAM
4-oz. can chopped GREEN CHILES
¼ tsp. coarsely-ground PEPPER
SALT to taste
¾ cup CHEDDAR CHEESE

Bake potatoes at 425 F for 40 to 50 minutes. Allow potatoes to cool, then cut in half.

In a bowl, mix sour cream, chiles, pepper, salt. Whip to a creamy texture.

Hollow out middle portion of each potato half and fill with sour cream mixture until well blended.

Spoon mixture into each potato. Garnish with grated cheddar cheese and heat in 350 F oven to allow cheese to melt. Serve hot. (Serves 4 to 6)

Nopalitos

Nopal (prickly pear cactus) is a common desert plant here in the Southwest. This recipe uses nopal in a red chile and cheese sauce. It can be served as a side dish or snack!

Nopal is available in stores ready-to-use, or you can cook your own. Since cacti come from the succulent family, they require light cooking only. Choose tender young leaflets which don't have spines. If they do have spines, they are very easily removed. Just scrape them off with a knife. Be sure to scrape away from you! Dice or chop before or after cooking.

3 Tbsp. OIL
3 Tbsp. FLOUR
2 cups MEAT BROTH
6 Tbsp. CHILI POWDER
1 cup cooked, diced NOPALES
½ cup grated LONGHORN CHEESE

In a skillet, make a basic chili sauce. Heat oil and brown flour. Dissolve chili powder in meat broth and blend into browned flour. Cook to a boil, then reduce heat to simmer. Add your favorite seasonings, as desired. Simmer 5 minutes, then add nopales and cheese. Allow cheese to melt. Serve warm. (Serves 4 to 5)

Nopales con Chile Verde (Cactus and Green Chile)

2 tsp. vegetable OIL
4 oz. cooked, diced GREEN CHILE
1 Tbsp. chopped ONION
1 large fresh TOMATO, chopped
SALT to taste
⅛ tsp. PEPPER
⅛ tsp. GARLIC POWDER
¾ cup diced, cooked NOPALES

Heat oil and saute green chile and onion. Add chopped tomato and season. Cover to simmer a few minutes, then blend in nopales. Cook for a few minutes. Serve. (Serves 4)

Salsas/Sauces

(A note on the words salsa and sauce; salsa is used to mean sauce so the words are interchangeable. There is so much overlapping of Spanish and English words, especially in border towns that a word can take on a variety of meanings. Mexicans, however, usually like thinner salsas for their enchiladas than Americans do.)

Table Salsa

Salsa is as common on Mexican tables as salt and pepper is! It is used for breakfast dishes, lunches and dinner dishes. Salsa is a combination of chiles and spices. It can be thick or thin, hot and spicy or mildly tasty. Here is a recipe for every day salsa used much in our house.

4 whole TOMATOES, chopped
1 JALAPEÑO CHILE, chopped
½ small ONION, chopped
6-oz. can TOMATO PASTE
1 minced CHILTEPIN
½ GARLIC CLOVE
¼ tsp. PEPPER
½ tsp. SALT
¼ tsp. PAPRIKA
1 Tbsp. VINEGAR

Mix all ingredients, adding seasonings last, in a blender. Mix for desired thickness. Salsa will keep for a week refrigerated in a closed container. We use glass jars.

Fresh Table Salsa

3 to 4 fresh TOMATOES, chopped
2 Tbsp. chopped ONION
2 cooked GREEN CHILES, diced
½ tsp. SALT
¼ tsp. coarsely ground PEPPER
2 dried fresh CILANTRO LEAVES, crushed

Mix in bowl. (Serves 2)

Salsa de Chile Verde

4 GREEN CHILES, cooked, diced
½ small ONION, chopped
4 to 5 fresh TOMATOES, chopped

Mix in bowl. Serve in salsa dish. Use stewed tomatoes, if desired. (Makes 5-6 servings)

Zesty Quick Salsa

1 thick ring of ONION, diced
3 small STEWED TOMATOES, chopped
4-oz. can diced GREEN CHILES
3 Tbsp. TOMATO PASTE (+ 1 tsp. if nec.)
⅛ tsp. GARLIC POWDER
SALT/PEPPER to taste

Mix diced onions and tomatoes in a bowl. Add chiles. Pour mixture into a saucepan and bring to a boil. Add 1 tablespoon tomato paste and stir. Then add 2 more tablespoons paste. (Add 1 teaspoon more for extra thickness.) Add seasonings. Reduce heat, cover, let simmer 10 minutes, stirring occasionally. (Makes one bowl of salsa)

Salsa Suave (Spicy Salsa)

2 oz. TOMATO PUREE
2 oz. diced GREEN CHILES
SALT/PEPPER
dash GARLIC POWDER
1 JALAPEÑO CHILE, diced
3 whole stewed TOMATOES, chopped
1 thick ring of ONION, chopped

Mix all ingredients in blender until well mixed. Makes 1½ cups. Refrigerate after use. Can be kept for up to a week in refrigerator if stored in glass container with lid.

Salsa Picante (Hot Salsa)

To make salsa picante, add 1 crushed chilitepin to other ingredients. This salsa is really hot!

Salsa de Chile Verde con Queso

1 tsp. OIL
4 to 5 fresh TOMATOES, chopped
4 large GREEN CHILES, cooked, diced
dash GARLIC POWDER
SALT/PEPPER to taste
6-oz. can TOMATO SAUCE
½ cup shredded LONGHORN CHEESE

In a saucepan, heat oil and saute tomatoes and chiles. Add seasonings. Stir in tomato sauce and cheese. Add water in small amounts for desired thickness. (If desired, saute 2 tablespoons diced onions.) Serve hot or cold. (Makes 5-6 servings)

Cheese Sauce

This is a basic recipe for cheese sauce. Add your favorite spices! This recipe goes well with meat and egg dishes. It serves well as a dip or dressing for raw vegetables.

2 cups cheddar or LONGHORN CHEESE, grated
6 Tbsp. OLIVE OIL
¼ tsp. SALT
¼ tsp. PEPPER
½ tsp. PAPRIKA
4-oz. can GREEN CHILES
1 Tbsp. VINEGAR
4 to 5 Tbsp. EVAPORATED MILK

Melt cheese in hot oil and add seasonings. Add chiles, vinegar and milk slowly while stirring. Heat to a bubbly boil. (Makes ¾ cup cheese sauce)

Salsa Rica

3 whole fresh TOMATOES, chopped
1 JALAPEÑO CHILE, chopped
1 small GREEN PEPPER, chopped
½ medium ONION, chopped
½ can TOMATO PASTE (6 oz.)
SALT/PEPPER/GARLIC POWDER to taste

Mix all ingredients in a blender and blend for desired thickness. Add seasonings. (Makes one bowl of salsa)

Enchilada Sauce #1

This is a basic recipe for enchilada sauce.

> 3 Tbsp. OIL
> 3 Tbsp. FLOUR
> 2 cups WATER (or use meat stock)
> 6 Tbsp. CHILI POWDER (homemade or store bought)
> 1 tsp. SALT
> ½ tsp. GARLIC POWDER

Heat oil and brown flour. To 2 cups of water (or stock) add chili powder and dissolve. Add chili to browned flour and mix well. Add seasonings and blend. Bring to a bubbly boil, stirring frequently. Simmer covered 5 minutes. (Makes 1¼ cups of sauce)

Enchilada Sauce with Cheese

Use the same ingredients for basic sauce but add ½ cup cheddar cheese and blend in after chili sauce boils. Melt cheese evenly. For a richer, smoother sauce, add ½ cup evaporated milk or so to chili. You can also add diced onions!

Salsa Sabrosa

> 3 to 4 chopped stewed TOMATOES
> 3 Tbsp. TOMATO PASTE
> 4 crushed CHILITEPINS
> 2 chopped, cooked GREEN CHILES
> 1 Tbsp. diced ONION
> 2 tsp. VINEGAR
> 1 tsp. crushed, fresh-dried CILANTRO
> ¼ tsp. SALT
> ⅛ tsp. GROUND PEPPER
> ⅛ tsp. GROUND CUMIN
> ⅛ tsp. GARLIC POWDER

In a bowl, mix tomatoes and tomato paste. Put in blender and mix. Add chilitepins, green chiles, onion, vinegar and mix. Add all seasonings and blend until smooth and thick. Makes 12 ounces of a delicious salsa to go with eggs, meats, and with chips as a zesty dip!

Avocado Sauce

Use this avocado sauce for chalupas, tacos or vegetables. It can be used as a dip, depending on its thickness.

2 Tbsp. LEMON JUICE (or lime juice)
4 Tbsp. EVAPORATED MILK
1 tsp. DRY MUSTARD
½ tsp. SALT
dash GARLIC SALT
PEPPER
1 Tbsp. minced PIMIENTOS
1 cup AVOCADOS, mashed

Mix juice, milk, add seasonings and blend well. Add avocados. Mix in blender for desired thickness. (Makes 1½ cups sauce)

Enchilada Sauce #2

2½ cups TOMATO SAUCE
1 Tbsp. TOMATO PASTE
¼ cup WATER
2 cooked, diced CHILES
2 Tbsp. diced ONION
pinch ground CUMIN
⅛ tsp. GARLIC POWDER
¼ tsp. GROUND PEPPER
SALT to taste

Combine ingredients in a saucepan. Heat to a bubbly boil, reduce heat, simmer 10-15 minutes. Stir frequently. (Makes 2½ cups)

Salsa Pronto (Quick Salsa)

2 Tbsp. salad OIL
2 Tbsp. diced ONION
1 minced GARLIC CLOVE
½ tsp. SALT
dash CAYENNE PEPPER
4 stewed TOMATOES, chopped
3 cooked GREEN CHILES, diced

Heat oil and soften onions, add minced garlic clove. Add salt and pepper, tomatoes and chiles. (Makes enough for 2 servings)

Salsa Picante

2 Tbsp. ONION, diced
2 tsp. SALAD OIL
4-oz. can GREEN CHILES, diced
2 JALAPEÑO CHILES, diced
3 Tbsp. TOMATO PASTE
SALT/PEPPER to taste
1 tsp. VINEGAR

Saute onion in oil, add green chiles and jalapeno chiles. Cook 2 minutes over medium heat, stirring frequently. Add tomato paste and stir in seasonings. (If salsa is too hot, add 1 teaspoon vinegar.) Stir and cover, cook 5 minutes. Leave covered to simmer. (Makes one bowl of salsa)

Meaty Salsa

1 Tbsp. OIL
2 Tbsp. diced ONION
2 large GREEN CHILES, chopped (cooked)
1 small JALAPEÑO CHILE, diced
6-oz. can TOMATO SAUCE
2 Tbsp. TOMATO PASTE
1 cup drained, cooked GROUND BEEF

Saute onions in oil until tender. Add chiles, tomato sauce and paste. Stir, bring to a boil. Slow cook over medium heat 5-8 minutes, covered. Add seasonings, simmer 5 minutes. Add meat. (Use as a dip with tortilla chips)

Taco Salsa

Use this salsa for tacos, egg dishes and burritos!

4 to 5 STEWED TOMATOES
4-oz. can diced GREEN CHILES
2 Tbsp. diced ONION
¼ tsp. SALT
½ tsp. OREGANO
dash GARLIC POWDER

Chop tomatoes into small pieces. Add green chiles, onions and seasonings. Makes one bowl of salsa.

Platillos de la Cena/ Main Dishes

Tacos #1

Just as corn tortillas are the bread of Mexican people, tacos are the best known and loved "sandwiches." They can be filled with cheese, beans, guacamole or with any chopped meat.

    1 lb. lean GROUND BEEF
    1 small diced ONION
    1 Tbsp. SALT
    ½ tsp. BLACK PEPPER
    ½ tsp. GARLIC POWDER
    6 to 8 ready-made TACO SHELLS
    shredded LETTUCE for garnish
    shredded CHEESE for garnish
    4 to 5 large stewed TOMATOES, chopped
    1 tsp. crushed OREGANO FLAKES

Brown meat first, then drain. Add onion and seasonings. Cook until onion is tender. Warm taco shells in oven or in a cooking pan with a cover.

In a bowl, mix tomatoes with oregano. When taco shells are warmed, fill with meat mixture and garnish with lettuce, tomato mixture and cheese. Serve with a side dish of refried beans or rice! (Makes 6 to 8 beef tacos)

Chorizo Tacos

Chorizo is spicy enough alone so that only lettuce and cheese are needed as garnish. If you use spicier chorizo, you can alternate cheese. In the taco shell, add a row of cheese, then chorizo, then cheese, top with lettuce and chopped stewed tomatoes if desired.

    1 lb. CHORIZO (home made or store bought)
    10 ready-made TACO SHELLS
    thinly-shredded LETTUCE
    1½ cups shredded LONGHORN CHEESE

Cook chorizo in a skillet and drain well. While chorizo is cooking, warm taco shells in oven or warmer. Add chorizo to each taco shell, then add lettuce and top with cheese. (Makes 10 delicious chorizo tacos)

Tacos #2

The more typical way of making tacos is to fry the corn tortilla while cooking the meat.

1 lb. lean GROUND BEEF
SALT/PEPPER
¼ tsp. GARLIC POWDER
8 CORN TORTILLAS
¼ cup vegetable OIL
shredded LETTUCE
shredded CHEESE
4 to 5 stewed TOMATOES, chopped
1 tsp. crushed OREGANO FLAKES

Take raw meat and season. Then, to each corn tortilla add a half-moon pattie of meat. Make sure meat is not too thick. Heat oil in a fry pan. Place tortilla meat-side up in the hot oil. Fold over half to make a taco shape. Fry until meat is cooked and tortilla is crispy brown. You can cook up to four tacos at a time. Keep oil hot so tacos won't be soggy.

Check for meat doneness by gently lifting tortilla with fork. Place cooked tacos in a paper towel-lined bowl. Add shredded lettuce, tomato and oregano mixture, shredded cheese and top with taco salsa! (Makes 8 beef tacos)

Spicy Beef Tacos

1 lb. GROUND BEEF
2 cans (8 oz.) TOMATO SAUCE
½ tsp. GARLIC POWDER
4 Tbsp. ONION FLAKES
½ tsp. CHILI POWDER
dash PEPPER
10 TACO SHELLS (ready-made shells)
1½ cups shredded LETTUCE
1 cup shredded CHEESE
1 cup chopped STEWED TOMATOES

Brown meat and drain. Stir in tomato sauce and all spices. Blend in well, simmer for 15 minutes. While meat is simmering, warm taco shells.

When meat is fully cooked and taco shells are fully heated, fill each taco shell with meat. Add lettuce, cheese, then spoon on tomatoes over cheese. (Makes 10 tacos!)

Bean Tacos

1 Tbsp. SALAD OIL (or peanut oil)
16-oz. can REFRIED BEANS
dash SALT
1 cup shredded CHEDDAR CHEESE
8 to 10 ready-made TACO SHELLS
thinly-shredded LETTUCE
TACO SALSA
4 Tbsp. chopped ONION for garnish

In a skillet, heat oil. Spoon in beans with a small amount of water to help soften them. Add salt. Heat beans.

When beans are fully heated, blend in shredded cheese and allow to melt. Add more cheese to thicken beans, as desired. Remove from heat and cover.

Warm taco shells in oven or warmer. Stir beans one last time, then fill warmed taco shells part way with beans. Top with lettuce, taco salsa, (use store bought or the **Taco Salsa** from **Salsa Section** in this book), add chopped onions over salsa as desired. (Makes 8 to 10 bean tacos)

Roast Beef Tacos

1 tsp. SALAD OIL
1½ lb. cooked, shredded ROAST BEEF
    (pressure cooked or crockpot cooked)
½ small ONION, chopped
½ tsp. GARLIC POWDER
¼ tsp. SALT
PEPPER (coarsely ground) as desired
3 to 4 chopped STEWED TOMATOES
pinch of OREGANO
8 to 10 ready-made TACO SHELLS
thinly-shredded LETTUCE
shredded CHEESE

In a skillet, heat oil and briskly saute roast beef. Break up strands of meat. Add onion and seasonings. Add tomatoes and oregano, heat until well blended. Cover and let simmer.

Warm taco shells. Fill taco shells with roast beef. Garnish with lettuce and shredded cheese. (Makes 8 to 10 tacos) Serve with refried beans or rice!

Tacos de Pollo (Chicken Tacos)

Make sure corn tortillas are fresh. Look for a soft texture, with no breaks, raised or crumbly edges. Corn tortillas should also be pliable.

> 1 fryer CHICKEN, stewed
> OIL for frying
> 12 CORN TORTILLAS
> 12 TOOTHPICKS
> shredded LETTUCE
> stewed TOMATOES
> ½ tsp. OREGANO
> JACK CHEESE, shredded
> canned small-size PEAS

Stew chicken until tender and it comes apart easily. (Don't over-cook!) Chicken stock can be freezer-kept for later cooking.

Bone chicken, separate into bite-size strips. Use all the chicken (except skin), place in bowl. Heat oil in frying pan, just enough to adequately fry.

Take a corn tortilla and at one end place a row of chicken pieces, "clump" into a row. Roll tortilla up snugly and insert a toothpick at the middle of the tortilla to keep closed for frying. Fry up to 6 tacos at a time to save cooking time.

As tacos are made, place in a bowl lined with paper towels to absorb oil. When you remove tacos from fry pan, allow oil to drain as needed. When tacos are done, garnish with finely-shredded lettuce, stewed tomatoes with oregano, shredded jack cheese and peas. Serve chicken tacos with rice and beans. (Serves 6)

● Once fried to crispy-brown, tacos should be removed with tongs or fork, suspended to drain for a few seconds, then placed in paper-towel-lined bowl.

● To drain tacos, when frying, tilt the fry pan and allow the oil to drain. Remove tacos with fork or tongs, suspend to drain, then place in a paper-towel-lined bowl.

● Vegetable oil, corn oil, safflower oil are all good choices for frying tacos, chimichangas, etc.

Frijoles al Horno (Baked Beans)

2 cups PINTO BEANS
1 Tbsp. SALT
1 quart WATER
½ lb. BACON
2 tsp. BACON FAT
1 medium ONION, chopped
2 medium TOMATOES, peeled, chopped finely
1 Tbsp. fresh, dried CILANTRO, crushed
¼ tsp. GARLIC POWDER
SALT/PEPPER to taste
½ cup shredded CHEESE

Rinse pinto beans and soak in cold water for 1 hour. Bring one quart of water to a boil, add pinto beans and salt. Cover to cook over medium heat until tender (1 hour, 30 minutes). (Beans need enough water to keep from becoming too dry, but drain water as needed to keep beans from becoming too "soupy.")

Cook bacon until crisp, drain. Break into bite-size pieces.

In a skillet, heat bacon fat and saute onion. Add chopped tomatoes, cilantro and seasonings. Blend well. Add bacon and cook for a few minutes.

Combine bacon mixture and partially-drained pinto beans. Cook to a boil, reduce heat and cook for 15 minutes, covered.

Preheat oven to 325 F. Lightly grease a shallow casserole dish. Turn beans into casserole dish and bake for 30 to 40 minutes. Garnish with shredded cheese, return to oven and bake an extra 5 minutes until cheese melts. (Serves 6)

Tocino y Frijoles (Beans and Bacon)

2 cups PINTO BEANS
1 1/3 quarts WATER
1 Tbsp. SALT

½ lb. BACON, sliced in half-slices
2 tsp. OREGANO FLAKES
1 GARLIC CLOVE

Inspect beans and remove any dark or broken beans. Rinse beans well under cold water.

In a cooking pot, bring water to a fast boil with salt. Add beans, bacon, oregano and garlic clove. Reduce heat to medium and cook until bacon is fully cooked and beans are tender (1 hour, 25 minutes). (Serves 6)

Meat Enchiladas

Meat enchiladas can be made with any meat. Serve with refried beans and Mexican rice.

Enchilada Sauce

3 Tbsp. OIL
3 Tbsp. FLOUR
2½ cups WATER
6 Tbsp. CHILI POWDER
¼ tsp. GARLIC POWDER
SALT to taste

To make the enchilada sauce, heat oil and brown flour in a saucepan. To water, add chili powder and dissolve evenly. Add to browned flour. Then add seasonings. Stir to boil over medium heat. Let simmer 10 to 15 minutes, cover.

Enchiladas

6 CORN TORTILLAS
OIL for softening tortillas
2 cups cooked lightly-seasoned GROUND BEEF,
   drained
sliced BLACK OLIVES
shredded CHEDDAR CHEESE
diced ONION

In a fry pan or skillet, heat enough oil to soften tortillas. Take one tortilla at a time and dip in the hot oil and soften lightly. Do not allow tortillas to become hardened. Place tortilla on a plate, then spread a lengthwise row of meat over one end of tortilla. Spread some enchilada sauce over the meat. Roll tortilla up singly. Add enchilada sauce over tortilla evenly. Repeat until tortillas and meat are all used.

Garnish with shredded cheese, diced onion and sliced black olives. (Makes 6 meat enchiladas)

● **Olive oil is preferred for sauteing onions, and for making enchilada sauce. It gives body and a smooth, rich taste to sauces.**

Cheese Enchiladas

A family favorite, enchiladas are a meal in themselves. They are easy to make and economical, too.

Enchilada Sauce

3 Tbsp. OIL
3 Tbsp. FLOUR
2 cups WATER
6 Tbsp. CHILI POWDER (mild)
¼ tsp. GARLIC POWDER
SALT to taste

Start with the enchilada sauce. In a medium saucepan, heat oil. Add flour and brown until light brown. To water add chili powder and stir until chili is dissolved evenly. Add the chili mixture and seasonings to the browned flour. Stir to boil over medium heat. Sauce should be of gravy-like consistency. Cover and leave nearby.

Enchiladas

3 to 4 Tbsp. cooking OIL
6 CORN TORTILLAS
1 cup grated CHEESE (white or longhorn)
1 small ONION, diced
thinly-shredded LETTUCE
½ cup sliced BLACK OLIVES

In a fry pan, heat oil. Lightly soften one corn tortilla at a time in the hot oil. Each side must be done. Place tortilla on plate quickly. (As you lift the tortilla from the oil, let drain as much as possible.) Sprinkle a lengthwise row of grated cheese toward one end of tortilla. Add a row of diced onion, then roll tortilla over snugly. Add chili sauce over tortilla to cover entire tortilla. Prepare all 6 tortillas in the same way. Garnish enchiladas with lettuce and black olives.

If enchiladas become cold during preparation, heat sauce and re-sauce them. Garnish just before serving. Side dishes for this Mexican favorite are rice and beans! (Makes 6 enchiladas)

For enchilada variations, try sour cream, chicken, roast beef, carne seca, ground beef for fillings. You can also use mild cheddar cheese and combinations of cheeses.

Sour Cream Chicken Enchiladas

2 (12½ oz.) cans CHUNK CHICKEN, well-drained
4-oz. can diced GREEN CHILES, well-drained
15-oz. can stewed, WHOLE TOMATOES,
　　drained and chopped
¼ tsp. SALT
⅛ tsp. ground PEPPER
1/3 cup vegetable OIL
1 dozen CORN TORTILLAS
16 oz. SOUR CREAM
2 tsp. PARSLEY FLAKES
SALT to taste
2 cups grated LONGHORN CHEESE
PARSLEY FLAKES as garnish

In a large mixing bowl, combine chicken, chiles and tomatoes. Blend well. Mix in salt and pepper. Lightly grease a square baking pan, approximately 14½ x 7½ x 1½. Preheat oven to 350 F. In a fry pan, heat oil. Have chicken mixture close at hand. Reduce heat to medium, then lightly soften each corn tortilla, one at a time. Lift from oil and let drain, using tongs or fork. Be careful not to tear tortillas. Place tortillas onto greased baking pan. Then at end of tortilla closer to you, spoon in 2 heaping tablespoons of the chicken mixture in a row. Roll tortilla up snugly. Repeat until all tortillas are filled.

In a mixing bowl, combine sour cream, parsley flakes and salt to taste. Mix well. Smooth sour cream mixture onto enchiladas. Spread as evenly as possible over surface and lightly spread sour cream over ends of enchiladas.

Sprinkle grated cheese over sour cream, then sprinkle with parsley flakes.

Cover with aluminum foil. Leave enough room to keep enchiladas from sticking. Bake for 30 to 35 minutes. Let cool for a few minutes, then serve. (Serves 6)

● **Longhorn cheese, Colby and Monterey Jack cheese melt quickly and smoothly. For cheese enchiladas, "Mexican White Cheese" (Queso Blanco) is a very good choice because it gives a distinct flavor. Cheeses which crumble easily are ideal for garnish.**

Sour Cream
Chicken Enchiladas Supreme

6 Tbsp. OIL
6 Tbsp. FLOUR
12 Tbsp. CHILI POWDER
1½ lb. CHICKEN (cooked, boned, skinned)
4 cups CHICKEN STOCK (saved from stewing)
½ tsp. GARLIC POWDER
SALT to taste
½ small ONION, diced
2 Tbsp. crushed, dried CILANTRO
1/3 cup sliced GREEN OLIVES
OIL for softening tortillas
12 CORN TORTILLAS
1 cup SOUR CREAM
1 cup grated LONGHORN CHEESE

In a saucepan, heat oil and brown flour. Dissolve chili powder in chicken stock from stewing chicken. (Make up difference with warm water, if you don't have 4 cups of stock). Season with garlic powder and salt. Bring to a boil, reduce heat, simmer, covered. Stir frequently until smooth and fairly thick.

In a bowl, shred chicken. Mix in onion, cilantro and green olives. Blend thoroughly. Salt to taste.

Heat oil in a fry pan to soften tortillas. Dip tortillas into hot oil lightly, do both sides. Place tortillas on plate and add a row (lengthwise) of chicken mixture. Roll tortilla up snugly. Repeat until all 12 tortillas are done.

Preheat oven to 350 F. Lightly grease a square casserole dish or cooking pan big enough to accommodate 12 enchiladas. Add a thin layer of enchilada sauce on the bottom of the baking dish and a little bit around the sides. Place all enchiladas on dish. Cover with aluminum foil and bake for 10 to 15 minutes until hot. Remove foil and top enchiladas with sour cream, evenly. Sprinkle with cheese, cover with foil and bake until cheese melts and enchiladas are bubbly hot.

Serve warm, two enchiladas per plate. (Serves 6)

Turkey Enchiladas

These delicious Turkey Enchiladas have a zesty avocado sauce.

2 Tbsp. BUTTER
2 cups cooked, diced TURKEY
1/3 cup diced BLACK OLIVES
¼ cup diced ONION
SALT to taste
¼ tsp. PEPPER
⅛ tsp. GARLIC POWDER
8 CORN TORTILLAS
OIL for softening tortillas
1 cup shredded MONTEREY JACK CHEESE

In a saucepan, melt butter. Add turkey and cook for a few minutes. Add olives, onion and seasonings. Blend well, cover, simmer 10 minutes. While turkey mixture is simmering, prepare sauce.

Avocado Sauce

1 cup mashed AVOCADO
4 to 5 Tbsp. EVAPORATED MILK
2 Tbsp. LEMON JUICE
1 tsp. DRY MUSTARD
½ tsp. SALT
dash GARLIC SALT
dash PEPPER

In a blender, add avocado, milk, lemon juice and mix once. Then add mustard and seasonings. Blend until creamy and fairly thick. Pour into bowl and leave nearby.

Return to turkey and stir briskly, place in dish. Preheat oven to 350 F. Lightly butter a shallow casserole dish. In a fry pan, heat 3 tablespoons oil, soften corn tortillas by dipping in hot oil (do both sides). Drain. Place quickly in casserole dish. Add turkey mixture, sprinkle with cheese, then roll tortilla up. Pour avocado sauce over it. Repeat until all corn tortillas are done. Pour remaining sauce over entire enchiladas. Heat in oven long enough to warm enchiladas. Serve 2 per plate. Top with sour cream and sliced black olives. (Serves 4)

Sonorenses
(Sonoran-Style Flat Enchiladas)

Good flat enchiladas should have a firm texture outside and be soft inside. Your fork should glide down your enchilada in its sauce! The secret to making good flat enchiladas is in the masa. Use masa harina (corn flour) and don't over-mix the masa. The masa should be pliable but not dough-like!

Enchiladas

3 cups MASA HARINA
1 tsp. BAKING POWDER
1 tsp. SALT
1 well-beaten EGG
2 cups MILK

In a large bowl, add all dry ingredients and mix. Add 1 cup of milk and egg, mix. Then add second cup of milk. When masa is too thick to mix with mixing spoon, take in your hands and form a ball. Masa should be pliable and slightly moist. Form 12 masa balls to make 3-inch circles. Try not to over-manipulate the masa. Take each masa ball and flatten with your hands. Work circle through with your fingers for even distribution of the masa. Use your fingers to make small indentations around the edge of the patties.

Put masa patties in a hot, oiled fry pan and fry until lightly brown. Turn pattie twice only. The longer you keep the pattie in the oil, the harder it will get. Cover patties in a lined bowl until sauce is prepared.

Enchilada Sauce

3 Tbsp. cooking OIL
3 Tbsp. FLOUR
2 cups WATER
6 Tbsp. CHILI POWDER
1 tsp. SALT
½ tsp. GARLIC POWDER

In a saucepan, heat oil and brown flour. Dissolve chili powder in water, then add to flour. Heat over medium heat until bubbly. Add seasoings. Sauce should be thick.

Pour hot enchilada sauce over enchilada patties. Serve 2 per plate and garnish with shredded cheese, diced onion, sliced green olives and thinly shredded lettuce.

Sonoran-Style Enchiladas

Here is a variation to rolled enchiladas. Sonoran-style enchiladas are stacked instead of rolled. You get more filling! Cut these enchiladas in half or quarters and serve with refried beans and Mexican rice!

Begin with the Enchilada Sauce:

Enchilada Sauce

5 to 6 Tbsp. SALAD OIL
6 Tbsp. FLOUR
1½ cups WATER (or meat stock)
6 to 8 level Tbsp. CHILI POWDER
½ tsp. SALT
¼ tsp. GARLIC POWDER
2/3 cup EVAPORATED MILK

In a saucepan, heat oil and brown flour. To water or meat stock, dissolve chili powder. Mix in with browned flour to make a gravy like mixture. Add salt and garlic powder. Heat to a bubbly boil, over medium heat. Stir in evaporated milk. Bring to a second boil. Cover, let simmer over low heat. (Makes 2 1/3 cups)

Enchiladas

8 CORN TORTILLAS
SALAD OIL for softening tortillas
2 cups cooked GROUND BEEF
1 small diced ONION
1 cup sliced BLACK OLIVES
2 cups grated JACK CHEESE

Heat oil in a skillet or fry pan and soften tortillas one at a time. Drain each tortilla as you remove it from the pan. Add some enchilada sauce on a large serving plate, then take a softened tortilla and place it on the sauce. Next, add ground beef, then onion, black olives and cheese. Repeat until you use up all the ingredients. Stack tortillas, then cut in half or quarters and serve a "stack" on each plate. Garnish with cheese if desired. (Serves 4)

Swiss Cheese Enchiladas

2 cups MEAT BROTH (or stock)
6 Tbsp. CHILI POWDER
4 Tbsp. vegetable OIL
4 Tbsp. FLOUR
½ tsp. OREGANO
¼ tsp. SALT
¼ cup vegetable OIL
8 CORN TORTILLAS
1½ cups shredded SWISS CHEESE
2/3 cup diced BLACK OLIVES
½ cup SOUR CREAM
½ cup chopped GREEN ONIONS

Dissolve chili powder in meat broth or stock. In a saucepan, heat oil and brown flour, blend in chili, add oregano and salt. Cook over medium heat until fairly thickened. Reduce heat, cover, let simmer.

Heat oil in a skillet, then soften corn tortillas one at a time. Dip in hot oil just long enough to soften them. Do both sides.

Place tortillas on plate, add a lengthwise row of cheese, sprinkle with olives and add a row of chili sauce. Roll tortilla up and pour chili sauce over it. Garnish with cream cheese and top with green onions. Serve immediately. (Serves 4)

● **To drain fat from fried foods, use soft paper towels or paper napkins.**

Green Corn Tamales

In the Southwest, green corn tamales are a seasonal treat. White field corn is usually available in late July, August and September. If you have a food processor, the corn can be ground quite easily. You can also use a food grinder or a blender to prepare the corn. It must be tender white corn ground finely to give a smooth, spreadable texture to your masa!

12 ears white, tender CORN (save husks)
1 cup MILK
1½ Tbsp. SALT
1 cup SHORTENING
½ cup MARGARINE (or butter)
2 cups grated LONGHORN CHEESE
12 ANAHEIM CHILES, fresh

Cut the ends of the corn with a sharp knife, then remove husks. Save all husks, remove corn silk and wash. Remove corn from cob with a large knife. Grind corn up as finely as possible in a food processor or blender. Take ground corn and place in a large mixing bowl. Add milk, salt, shortening, butter or margarine and mix. In a blender, blend at high speed, adding small amount of milk if corn becomes dry. (With a food processor, add corn and rest of ingredients and process.)

When corn mixture is well mixed, place in large mixing bowl once again. Add cheese, blend in using a large mixing spoon. Corn mixture should have a smooth and spreadable texture. This will be the "masa," although it will be moister and fluffier than regular masa.

Roast green chiles in oven 350 F until fully roasted. Remove skin, seed, wash chiles and cut into long strips. (You can also use canned chiles.)

Choose the larger husks you saved and rinse in cold water. Drain excess water. Now, prepare to do the spreading.

Using a tablespoon, spoon corn mixture (masa) on wider end of corn husks. Spread evenly but not thickly to cover most of the corn husk but not the narrow end or tail of the husk. Add strips of chiles and if desired sprinkle 1 tablespoon of grated longhorn cheese over chiles. Roll husk to cover masa and chiles and tuck husk tail up. Set upright so that masa shows. Repeat until all the masa is used.

Cook tamales in a steamer or a large cooking pot. If you use a cooking pot, line pot with aluminum foil or extra corn husks. Place tamales in upright position with a crumpled ball of foil at the center of the pot to help hold tamales in place. Add tamales over each other so they hold each other up. Add 1 cup of water carefully to side of pot. Try not to get tamales wet. Let boil, covered, then cook over medium heat for 45 minutes to an hour. Check tamales every 20 minutes and add ½ cup water or so to keep tamales from becoming too dry. Tamales are ready when they are easily removed from the husk. (Makes 30 tamales) Total preparation time: 2½ hours.

Chicken Tamale Pie

Crust

1¼ cups MASA HARINA MIX
2/3 cup WATER
2 Tbsp. OIL
2 tsp. CHILI POWDER
¾ tsp. SALT

For the crust, combine all the ingredients above in a mixing bowl. When well mixed, line a buttered 1½-quart casserole dish with the masa. Line evenly, bottom and sides.

Filling

2 to 2½ cups COOKED CHICKEN, diced
1 small ONION, chopped
1 minced GARLIC CLOVE
½ tsp. THYME
1 tsp. SALT
⅛ tsp. PEPPER
15-oz. can CREAM-STYLE CORN
4-oz. can chopped GREEN CHILES
½ cup sliced BLACK OLIVES
½ cup PIMIENTOS, chopped
1 cup shredded, sharp CHEDDAR CHEESE

In a saucepan, add chicken, onion, garlic and seasonings. Saute in a small amount of oil until onion is tender. Add rest of ingredients for filling (except for cheese), and blend in well. Cook for a few minutes, then cover and let simmer.

Preheat oven to 375 F. Add filling to masa-lined casserole dish. Bake for 20 minutes. Sprinkle with cheese and allow cheese to melt. When cheese is melted, remove from oven, let stand for a few minutes, then serve. (Serves 6 to 8)

Chicken Tamales

Meat

3 lbs. CHICKEN
3 quarts WATER
2 tsp. SALT
GARLIC CLOVE, whole
small whole ONION

Masa

3 cups MASA HARINA
1 cup SHORTENING
2 cups CHICKEN STOCK (saved from stewing)

Chili

5 to 6 Tbsp. cooking OIL
6 Tbsp. FLOUR
12 Tbsp. CHILI POWDER, mild
4 cups CHICKEN STOCK (saved from stewing)
½ tsp. SALT
¼ tsp. PEPPER
¼ tsp. GARLIC POWDER
1 cup BLACK OLIVES, pitted
1 to 2 bags dry CORN HUSKS

Place chicken in a Dutch oven with water, add salt, garlic clove and onion. Stew until skin is easily removed from chicken. Remove garlic clove and onion. Bone chicken, remove skin, drain and save all stock. Dice chicken, return to Dutch oven.

In a large mixing bowl, combine masa harina, shortening and chicken stock. Knead masa until it is smooth and "spreadable." To test masa after kneading, fill a glass with water and drop a bit of masa in it. If masa floats, it is ready to use.

Heat oil and brown flour. Dissolve chili powder in chicken stock (make up difference with water if you run out of stock). Add to browned flour. Mix, bring to a fast boil. Reduce heat and add seasonings. Add chili mixture to chicken in Dutch oven. Cover and let simmer 15 minutes.

Soak dry corn husks to soften them. Some people soak them overnight. Drain husks over a rack.

Take husks to where masa is and have chili at hand. Pick bigger husks. Then, with a spoon, spread masa over the wider bottom part of husk. Hold husk in your palm while spreading masa. Spoon 1 to 2 tablespoons of chili mixture over masa, then add black olives. Fold over sides of husk snugly and pull "tail" of husk up. Set tamales in an upright position in a cooking pot lined with aluminum foil or a steamer. Steam-cook tamales until the masa is easily removed from the husk. (Makes 1 dozen tamales)

Zesty Tamale Pie

(Tia Elena's Recipe)

Here is my favorite "home" recipe from my Aunt Elena.

Crust

2¾ cups COLD WATER
1 tsp. SALT
2 tsp. CHILI POWDER
1½ cups CORN MEAL

Combine all ingredients (but leave ½ cup cornmeal aside for topping) in a saucepan and cook over medium heat for 10 to 15 minutes, until thick but not dry. Line sides and bottom of buttered casserole dish (1½-quart) thinly with cornmeal mixture.

Filling

1 to 1½ lbs. GROUND BEEF
1 small chopped ONION
1 minced GARLIC CLOVE
1 tsp. SALT
½ tsp. OREGANO
can creamed-style CORN
4-oz. can diced CHILES
2 medium, diced, JALAPEÑO CHILES
small can sliced BLACK OLIVES
1 cup shredded, sharp CHEDDAR CHEESE

In medium saucepan, over medium heat, cook ground beef until brown. Add onion and cook until tender. Then drain meat well to remove excess oils. Add garlic clove to meat and cook for 2 minutes, then add salt, oregano and corn. Remove from heat and add chiles and black olives. Pour meat mixture in your casserole dish. Sprinkle the cornmeal mixture over casserole evenly. Then add the shredded cheese over top. Bake in 350 F oven for 35 to 40 minutes until cheese is melted completely. (Serves 6 to 8)

Beef-Enchilada Casserole

1½ to 2 lbs. lean GROUND BEEF
1 crushed GARLIC CLOVE
4 to 5 STEWED TOMATOES, chopped
6 oz. TOMATO SAUCE
2 tsp. OLIVE OIL
3 Tbsp. diced ONION
SALT to taste
coarsely-ground PEPPER
6 to 8 JALAPEÑOS, diced
12 CORN TORTILLAS, cut in ¼ triangles
3 cups shredded CHEDDAR CHEESE
1/3 cup fresh CILANTRO, cut in small pieces
1 cup grated JACK CHEESE (or parmesan)

In a skillet, brown meat, then drain well. Return meat to skillet, add crushed garlic clove and cook until well-blended into meat. Cover, leave aside.

In a saucepan, add stewed tomatoes, tomato sauce, olive oil, onion and all seasonings. Bring to a boil, reduce heat, cover to simmer 20 minutes, stir frequently. Blend in jalapeños, cover, put aside.

Preheat oven to 350 F, then lightly butter a square 2-quart casserole dish. Cut corn tortillas into quarters. To cheddar cheese, blend in cilantro.

In a mixing bowl, combine cooked meat and sauce, mix well. Layer casserole dish with tortillas, then add meat/sauce mixture. Sprinkle with cheddar cheese/cilantro mixture, then add another layer of tortillas and repeat, ending with meat mixture. Sprinkle entire casserole with jack cheese and any leftover cheddar cheese. Bake for 35 to 40 minutes until cheese is completely melted. (Serves 6 to 8)

● A bulb of garlic is composed of several garlic cloves, each of which can be separated from the cluster.

● Garlic cloves can be minced or crushed. Peel outer skin and use only a few until the desired taste is achieved.

Tostadas

OIL for frying
6 CORN TORTILLAS
16-oz. can REFRIED BEANS
finely-shredded LETTUCE
1 cup shredded CHEESE
½ cup sliced GREEN OLIVES
¼ cup diced ONION (optional)
¼ tsp. OREGANO/dash GARLIC POWDER
4 to 5 chopped STEWED TOMATOES

In a skillet, fry corn tortillas until crisp and golden brown. Place fried tortillas in a bowl lined with paper towels.

In a saucepan, heat 1 tablespoon oil and add beans, add small amount of water, mash beans well. Allow beans to come to a boil, then place in a bowl. Have lettuce, cheese, onion, olives at hand.

Add oregano and garlic powder to chopped tomatoes. Blend well.

Take a fried corn tortilla and spoon beans over it. Sprinkle onions over beans, then lettuce, tomato with seasonings, cheese and lastly, sliced green olives. (Makes 6)

Variations

On beans, add slices of avocado, ground beef, slices of hard boiled egg, sour cream, salsa, turkey, ham, chorizo, chicken.

Mexican Pepper Steak

1½ lb. ROUND STEAK, tenderized
2 Tbsp. SALAD OIL
½ small ONION, coarsely chopped
1 Tbsp. FLOUR
2 fresh GREEN CHILES, sliced in rings
¼ cup MEAT JUICES (saved from cooking meat)
½ cup WATER

Cut steak into thin strips, then brown in a skillet. Save ¼ cup meat juices. Put steak strips in a bowl, then, using the same skillet, heat oil and saute onion. Add flour to this and brown. Add chiles and cook until onion is tender. Blend in meat juices and water. Mix well. Add meat, cover and simmer 20 minutes until green chiles are tender. (Makes 4 to 5 servings) Serve this tasty dish with refried beans and warm flour tortillas.

Meat Tostadas

Serve meat tostadas with refried beans for a satisfying dinner!

OIL for frying
8 CORN TORTILLAS
2 tsp. SALAD OIL
2½ to 3 cups cooked GROUND BEEF
3 Tbsp. diced ONION
½ cup fresh TOMATO, chopped
2 diced GREEN CHILES, cooked
shredded LETTUCE
4 to 5 stewed TOMATOES, chopped
shredded CHEESE, Monterey jack or cheddar

Fry corn tortillas until golden brown, drain and place in lined container.

In a skillet, heat oil, add ground beef, onion, tomato, green chiles and saute until mixture is well heated. Cover, reduce heat, let simmer for 10 minutes.

Take each fried corn tortilla and top with meat mixture. Spread evenly over tortilla. Add shredded lettuce, chopped stewed tomatoes, and garnish with cheese. (Serves 4)

Tostadas de Guacamole

OIL for frying
8 CORN TORTILLAS
GUACAMOLE*
2 cooked CHILES, sliced
½ cup shredded CHEESE garnish

In a fry pan, heat oil and fry corn tortillas until crisp and golden brown. Place fried tortillas in a bowl lined with paper towels.

Take each fried tortilla and spread Guacamole* evenly over tortilla. Garnish with slices of green chiles and sprinkles of cheese. (Serves 4)

*Guacamole

2 large AVOCADOS, mashed
1 tsp. LEMON JUICE
1 Tbsp. diced ONION
1 Tbsp. PIMIENTOS
1 small TOMATO, diced
SALT to taste
dash PEPPER
dash GARLIC SALT

Mix all ingredients in a blender and mix fairly thick. (Makes 2½ cups, approximately)

Picadillo (Minced Meat)

Picadillo can be made in a variety of ways with different ingredients. In Cuba, the dish is served with fried bananas. Picadillo is used as a filling in pies or turnovers, as an appetizer, a spread or an entree.

¼ cup OLIVE OIL
1 small ONION, chopped
1 small GREEN PEPPER, chopped
3 crushed GARLIC CLOVES
1 cup TOMATO SAUCE
2 oz. TOMATO PUREE
1 tsp. VINEGAR
1 Tbsp. SALT
½ tsp. CAYENNE PEPPER
1 lb. cooked GROUND BEEF
½ lb. cooked PORK, chopped
½ cup DRY WHITE WINE
1/3 cup RAISINS
¼ cup chopped BLACK OLIVES
¼ cup chopped PECANS
1/3 cup cooked MUSHROOMS

Heat oil and saute onion, green pepper and garlic. Add tomato sauce and puree. Cook for 1 to 2 minutes. Add vinegar, salt and pepper. Add beef and pork. Cook for 5 to 8 minutes. Add remaining ingredients. Cook over medium heat until liquid evaporates and meat is well cooked. (Serves 6)

● Except when frying is recommended, cooking should be done over low heat.

● Masa Harina (dehydrated corn flour) can be used as a substitute for fresh masa.

● Peeled garlic cloves can be used whole when stewing meats or cooking salsas or sauces. Remove cloves before serving.

Flautas de Pollo (Chicken Flautas)

Flautas are "rolled" tacos with a non-chili sauce or dressing over them and a meat mixture or other mixed filling.

4 Tbsp. BUTTER
¼ cup FLOUR
2 Tbsp. finely-diced ONION
1 Tbsp. SALAD OIL
⅛ tsp. PAPRIKA
SALT/PEPPER to taste
1 cup cooked, diced CHICKEN
2 Tbsp. LEMON JUICE
½ cup chopped BLACK OLIVES
OIL for frying
12 CORN TORTILLAS
TOOTHPICKS

In saucepan, heat butter, add flour, stir, saute onion, add oil. Stir in seasonings, lemon juice, and black olives. Heat 2 minutes, then add diced chicken. Stir in small amounts of hot water as needed to keep mixture moist but not overly moistened. Mixture should be slightly dry for flauta filling. Set aside covered for a few minutes. Place in bowl, mix well.

Heat oil in a deep fryer skillet. Fill corn tortillas with one tablespoon chicken mixture. Roll tortilla up snugly and hold in place with toothpick. Place in skillet and fry for 1 to 2 minutes. Do both sides of tortilla. Do not allow tortilla to become crispy-fried, just browned and softened. Fry several tortillas at a time. Set quick-fried tortillas in bowl with paper towels and remove toothpicks.

Sour Cream Sauce

2 Tbsp. SUGAR
¼ tsp. SALT
dash CAYENNE PEPPER
1 cup SOUR CREAM
2 Tbsp. LEMON JUICE
1 Tbsp. minced PIMIENTO
CHIVES for garnish

Make a sour cream sauce after tortillas are done. In a bowl, mix sugar, salt, pepper into a cup of sour cream, add juice and pimientos. Whip up to a fluffy texture.

Spoon sour cream sauce over hot flautas, two flautas per plate. Garnish with chives, serve with beans and a small salad. (Serves 6)

Chicken Casserole

2 cups cooked EGG NOODLES
2 Tbsp. BUTTER
2 tsp. SALAD HERBS
1/3 cup PARMESAN CHEESE
2 tsp. OLIVE OIL
2 Tbsp. diced ONION
1 minced GARLIC CLOVE
1 large TOMATO, chopped
4 sliced GREEN CHILES, cooked
½ cup sliced MUSHROOMS, cooked
½ tsp. SALT
¼ tsp. PEPPER (coarsely ground)
⅛ tsp. ground THYME
⅛ tsp. PAPRIKA
½ cup CHICKEN STOCK (or chicken broth)
1½ cups cooked CHICKEN, cut in strips
    (or canned chunk chicken)
2 cups sharp CHEDDAR CHEESE, shredded
2 Tbsp. finely-diced PIMIENTO

Drain and butter the cooked egg noodles, while still warm. Sprinkle in salad herbs and parmesan cheese. Blend in well and cover, put aside.

In a saucepan, heat olive oil and saute onion and garlic. Add chopped tomato, green chiles and mushrooms. Mix in salt, pepper, thyme and paprika. Add chicken stock (saved from cooking chicken) and chicken strips. Simmer for 10 to 15 minutes, stirring occasionally, cover.

After simmering, combine chicken and noodles, add 1½ cups cheese and pimientos, mix in well. Preheat oven to 350 F. Butter a 1½-quart casserole dish. Put mixture in dish and top with remaining ½ cup of cheese. Bake for 10 to 15 minutes, until cheese melts completely. (Serves 4 to 6)

● When stewing chicken, beef or fish, save the stock in a freezer-safe container to use later. Stock gives dishes a full-bodied taste.

Pollo Especial (Special Chicken)

6 whole CHICKEN BREASTS
1 cup MILK
½ cup HALF AND HALF
½ cup CHICKEN STOCK
4 to 6 JALAPEÑO CHILES, cut in strips
½ cup sliced OLIVES
⅛ tsp. SWEET BASIL
¼ tsp. OREGANO
¼ tsp. coarsely-ground PEPPER
SALT to taste
dash GARLIC POWDER
½ small RED ONION, chopped

Remove skin from each chicken breast. Rinse, then place in a cooking pot with enough water to cover chicken. Stew, covered, until chicken is tender and fully cooked. Save stock.

In a saucepan, heat milk, half and half, and chicken stock you saved from stewing. Let simmer, covered. Cut jalepeños into thin strips, remove stems and seeds.

In a bowl, add jalapeños, then olives and all seasonings. Mix well. Preheat oven to 350 F and lightly butter a shallow casserole dish. Add chile mixture to milk mixture, blend well. Add chopped onion.

Place chicken breasts in casserole dish and pour sauce over all evenly. Bake for 20 minutes. Serve with sauce. (Serves 6)

Pollo Cocido (Chicken Stew)

2 to 2½ lbs. CHICKEN, separated in pieces
2 Tbsp. (or so) BUTTER
1 GARLIC CLOVE minced

1 cup WATER   ⅛ tsp. CAYENNE PEPPER
2 tsp. OLIVE OIL   ½ tsp. SALT
½ cup chopped CELERY ½ tsp. PAPRIKA

4 whole GARLIC CLOVES
⅛ tsp. CUMIN
1 BAY LEAF
1 to 2 sliced CARROTS
½ cup diced GREEN PEPPERS
½ small ONION, cut in thin rings

Rinse chicken in cold water. Separate into pieces. Blanch chicken in hot water, then blot dry. Butter each chicken piece, then sprinkle with minced garlic. Work garlic into chicken, rubbing it in.

To crockpot, add water and olive oil and all seasonings. Place chicken in crockpot. Add carrots, green peppers, onion and celery. Cook covered until chicken is tender and is easily removed from bone. Low heat for 6-8 hours and high heat 3-5 hours is the cooking time for most crockpot dishes. Check chicken while it is stewing and baste it so seasonings are distributed.

When chicken is fully cooked, bone before serving, if desired, and serve with broth. Serve with potatoes and biscuits. (Serves 6)

Chicken Enchilada Casserole

2 Tbsp. BUTTER
1½ lbs. shredded cooked CHICKEN
½ small ONION, diced
6 to 8 JALAPEÑO CHILES, diced
⅓ cup HALF AND HALF
SALT to taste
coarsely-ground PEPPER
¼ tsp. GARLIC SALT
large pinch OREGANO
½ tsp. PAPRIKA
3 cups JACK CHEESE, grated
12 CORN TORTILLAS, cut in quarters
2/3 cup grated CHEDDAR (or longhorn) CHEESE
SLICED BLACK OLIVES, garnish

In a skillet, melt butter and briefly saute shredded chicken. Add onion and diced chiles. Cook for a few minutes. Cover, set aside.

In a saucepan, heat half and half, stir in seasonings, bring to a slow boil. Add chicken mixture, blend thoroughly, cover and simmer for a few minutes.

Preheat oven to 350 F. Lightly grease a 2-quart casserole dish and line with corn tortilla triangles. Then add portion of chicken over tortillas, sprinkle with jack cheese, add another layer of tortillas, then repeat until all ingredients are used up.

Transfer casserole into greased dish, sprinkle with cheese and bake for 35 minutes. Garnish with sliced black olives, return casserole to oven, shut oven and leave for 5 minutes. Serve warm. (Serves 6 to 8)

Chicken Mole

6 whole CHICKEN BREASTS
8 to 10 dried CHILES, combinations, mostly mild
6 Tbsp. VEGETABLE OIL
¾ cup WATER
2 Tbsp. chopped ONION
1 diced GARLIC CLOVE
1 medium TOMATO, chopped
2 toasted BREAD slices, cut in cubes
2 Tbsp. RAISINS (or dates)
2 Tbsp. PEANUTS
½ tsp. ground CINNAMON
¼ tsp. ground CLOVES
3 to 4 cups CHICKEN BROTH
2 Tbsp. COCOA
2 tsp. SUGAR
SALT to taste

Remove skin from chicken breasts and rinse chicken. Place in cooking pot or Dutch oven and cover with water. Put cover on pot, and stew, cooking until tender. Remove stock and pass through a sieve, leaving stock at hand. Place chicken aside.

Remove stems from dried chiles and break into small pieces. Fry in 3 tablespoons oil for a few minutes. Drain. Put chiles in blender with approximately ¾ cup water and puree. Pass through a sieve for a smooth paste. Place aside.

In a blender, puree onion, garlic and tomato. In a saucepan, heat 1 tablespoon oil and saute bread cubes. Add bread to onion mixture with raisins, peanuts, cinnamon and cloves. Puree.

Heat 2 tablespoons oil and cook onion mixture over medium heat for 8 minutes. Add chili puree and cook 5 minutes. Blend in 3 to 4 cups chicken broth/stock. Add cocoa, sugar and salt. Cover to simmer 1½ hours, stirring occasionally. Then cook uncovered until thick. You should have a fairly thick mole.

Preheat oven to 350 F and lightly butter a square casserole dish. Place chicken breasts and pour mole over all. Bake for 10 to 15 minutes, long enough for chicken to be fully heated. (Serves 6)

● Semi-sweet chocolate can be substituted for cocoa. Use a one-ounce square of chocolate for cocoa in this recipe. Chocolate must be melted before using.

Arroz con Pollo (Chicken and Rice)

Using fresh chicken stock is a *must* for truly delicious rice. So always stew chicken and save the broth. Remember, you can freeze broth. Seal in a plastic, air tight container.

Chicken Broth

1 2/3 quarts WATER
2½ to 3 lb. fryer CHICKEN
1 minced GARLIC CLOVE
1 tsp. SALT
1 BAY LEAF

In a 2-quart cooking pot, add water to chicken, bring to a quick boil, leave covered. Add minced garlic clove, salt and bay leaf and cook chicken over medium heat, covered, until chicken is tender. Add hot water in small amounts if needed during cooking. Save chicken broth (4 to 5 cups). When chicken is cooked, bone and dice 2 cups of chicken, set aside.

Chicken and Rice

3 Tbsp. SALAD OIL
½ lb. long-grain white RICE
2 Tbsp. chopped ONION
3 Tbsp. diced GREEN PEPPER
4 to 5 cups CHICKEN STOCK (saved from cooking)
½ tsp. PEPPER
½ tsp. SALT
dash GARLIC SALT
6-oz. can TOMATO SAUCE
1 cup WATER (hot)
2 cups diced CHICKEN

Heat oil in skillet, add rice and brown over medium heat. Saute onions and green peppers until tender. Add chicken stock, salt, pepper and garlic salt. Mix well. Then add tomato sauce. Cook rice over medium heat for 45 to 50 minutes. Leave covered and stir occasionally. Add 1 cup hot water if rice becomes dry.

When rice is tender, add chicken and mix well. Leave covered until ready to serve. (Serves 6)

Paella

The people of a small town in Spain heard news that her majesty the Queen would be passing their way. They decided to fix a very special dish for her, but couldn't decide on a name. Time grew short, and they decided to call the dish "For Her" *(Para Ella)*. Over the years, the dish became known as paella, a dish first made for a queen!

2 to 2½ cups diced, cooked CHICKEN
OIL
1 medium ONION, finely-chopped
4 to 5 large STEWED TOMATOES, chopped
1 large GREEN PEPPER, seeded and chopped
2 tsp. SALT
2 tsp. PAPRIKA
½ tsp. black PEPPER
dash CAYENNE
large pinch of powdered SAFFRON
1 crushed GARLIC CLOVE
2½ to 3 cups CHICKEN BROTH
2 cups pre-cooked long-grain RICE
1 cup PEAS
1 cup cooked SHRIMP, shelled and deveined
4-oz. can sliced GREEN CHILES
PARSLEY
BLACK OLIVES

Stew a fryer chicken until tender-firm and save broth. Bone chicken into bite-size pieces.

Heat oil in Dutch oven and briskly saute. Add onion and chopped stewed tomatoes, chopped green pepper. Add all seasonings and mix.

To the chicken broth, add the crushed garlic clove and rice. Then add this mixture to Dutch oven and stir thoroughly.

Cook over medium heat in Dutch oven, covered, stirring occasionally for 45 minutes to 1 hour. Add peas, shrimp and green chiles last 10 minutes of cooking time. Simmer over low heat for 15 minutes. Garnish with parsley and sliced black olives before serving. (Serves 6)

Chicken Tortilla Casserole

2 cups cooked elbow MACARONI
1 cup EVAPORATED MILK
1 Tbsp. PARSLEY FLAKES
1 tsp. OREGANO
2 cups cooked, diced CHICKEN
8 CORN TORTILLAS, diced
1 tsp. SALT
⅛ tsp. PEPPER
¼ tsp. GARLIC SALT
2 cups grated CHEDDAR CHEESE
2 Tbsp. BUTTER

In a mixing bowl, combine macaroni, ½ cup milk, parsley flakes and oregano. Add chicken, diced tortillas and all seasonings. Mix in remaining ½ cup milk.

Sprinkle in cheese, distributing evenly.

Preheat oven to 350 F. Butter 1½-quart casserole dish and pour in chicken mixture. Bake for 20 minutes until cheese is bubbly. Serve hot. (Serves 5 to 6)

Stuffed Tomatoes

2 Tbsp. BUTTER
2 Tbsp. minced ONION
3 Tbsp. diced GREEN PEPPER
4-oz. can diced GREEN CHILES
2 cups cooked, diced CHICKEN
1 cup soft BREAD CRUMBS
½ tsp. SALT
⅛ tsp. PEPPER
¼ tsp. PAPRIKA
6 large, firm TOMATOES

In a saucepan, melt butter and saute onion, green pepper and chiles. When onion and green pepper are tender, add chicken. Mix well, then add bread crumbs and seasonings. Blend thoroughly and cover, simmer 10 minutes.

Wash and hollow tomatoes. Take chicken mixture and fill tomatoes. Heat oven to 375 F. Grease a baking dish and place stuffed tomatoes. Bake for 25 to 30 minutes. Serve with rice! (Serves 6)

Chicken Burros

2 Tbsp. BUTTER
1 minced GARLIC CLOVE
2 Tbsp. diced ONION
3 stewed TOMATOES, chopped
¼ tsp. PAPRIKA
SALT to taste
PEPPER as desired
2 cups cooked, diced CHICKEN
¼ cup BLACK OLIVES
4 to 5 FLOUR TORTILLAS (burrito size)

In a saucepan, melt butter, add garlic and onion. Saute onion until tender. Add tomatoes and seasonings.

Add chicken and black olives, blend in well. Simmer, covered, 10 to 15 minutes. Chicken filling should be slightly dry. Cook uncovered for a few minutes.

Warm tortillas on both sides. Add chicken filling to tortillas, roll over then tuck up bottom end. Serve with any salsa or use the **Fresh Table Salsa** (salsa section). (Makes 4 to 5 burros)

Arroz y Pollo al Horno
(Chicken and Rice Casserole)

Baked rice and chicken is a delicious variation to the skillet version. Use a heavy casserole dish to keep rice from becoming too dry!

3 Tbsp. BUTTER
1 small ONION, coarsely chopped
2½ cups CHICKEN STOCK
½ tsp. SALT
¼ tsp. PEPPER
¼ tsp. GARLIC SALT
1 cup cooked, long-grain RICE
2 cups cooked, diced CHICKEN
4-oz can sliced MUSHROOMS, undrained

In a saucepan, melt butter and saute onions. Add chicken stock and seasonings. Turn heat off and cover.

In a casserole dish, combine rice and chicken. Add chicken stock mixture and undrained mushrooms. Mix well. Preheat oven to 375 F. Cover casserole and bake for 35 minutes. Then remove cover and mix. Bake 10 more minutes.

Fluff rice/chicken before serving. (Serves 4 to 6)

Burros

Burros are rolled flour tortillas filled with meat or beans, garnished with salsa!

Typical fillings for burros include: refried beans, red chili con carne, ground beef, carne seca, green chili con carne or a combination of beans and red chili con carne. Burros can also be filled with egg, chorizo, jam, jelly or cheese. Twelve-inch size flour tortillas are used most often, but the bigger the flour tortillas, the bigger your burros!

Bean Burros

1 tsp. SALAD OIL
15-oz. can REFRIED BEANS
4 FLOUR TORTILLAS (12-inch)
shredded CHEESE
SALSA for garnish

In a small skillet, heat oil and add beans. Mash and heat until bubbly. Add a small amount of water. Cook beans, stirring frequently. Warm tortillas, then when beans are ready, spoon a row of beans on the lower end of the tortilla. Sprinkle with cheese, roll tortilla up snugly and garnish with salsa. (Makes 4 burros)

Combination Burros

In the Southwest, combination burros feature a red chili meat mixture joined by delicious refried beans.

use recipe for CHILI CON CARNE
1 Tbsp. OIL
8-oz. can REFRIED BEANS
6 FLOUR TORTILLAS
LETTUCE, shredded
3 to 4 chopped STEWED TOMATOES
⅛ cup fresh, dried, crushed CILANTRO

Follow recipe for **Chili con Carne.** Then, in a skillet, heat oil and beans. Add small amount of water to help cook beans.

Warm tortillas, then take one tortila, add a row of beans (they should be thickish) near the bottom end of the tortilla. Add a row of chili con carne next to the row of beans. Fold over the two sides of the tortilla, then roll up the bottom end snugly to make a burro. Repeat with all tortillas.

Garnish each burro with lettuce topped with chopped stewed tomatoes. Sprinkle with cilantro. (Makes 6 hefty combination burros)

Red Chili Burro #1

1½ lbs. BRISKET
WATER for stewing brisket
2 Tbsp. SHORTENING
3 Tbsp. FLOUR
1 cup MEAT STOCK (saved from stewing)
3 Tbsp. CHILI POWDER
¼ tsp. GARLIC SALT
⅛ tsp. ground CUMIN
SALT to taste
6 FLOUR TORTILLAS (burro size)
shredded LETTUCE and grated CHEESE, garnish

Cook brisket until well-done. Add enough water to cooking pot to cover meat. When meat is fully-cooked let cool, then shred into thin strands.

In a skillet, heat shortening and brown flour. To meat stock saved from stewing, dissolve chili powder, then add to skillet with browned flour. Season with garlic salt, cumin and salt to taste. Heat to a bubbly boil, reduce heat, let simmer 10 minutes.

Warm tortillas. Add chili/meat mixture to each tortilla and wrap up into burro. Serve with refried beans! (Makes 6)

Green Chili Burros

1½ lbs. BRISKET (or chuck roast), stewed
2 Tbsp. OIL
¼ tsp. GARLIC SALT
pinch OREGANO
SALT to taste
⅛ tsp. ground CILANTRO
3 Tbsp. chopped ONION
4-oz. can cooked CHILES, cut in strips
6 FLOUR TORTILLAS (burro size)

Before stewing meat, remove all visible fat. Stew until fully cooked. When cool, shred or cut into bite-size strips.

In a skillet, heat 2 tablespoons of oil, then combine meat and all seasonings. Cook for 2 minutes over high heat, stirring constantly. Allow meat to become dry. Reduce heat, add onion. Cover, simmer 10 minutes. Add chiles, blend in well.

Warm tortillas. When meat is fully heated, add meat to tortillas and wrap into burros.

(Makes 6 delicious green chili burros) Garnish burros with salsa.

Green Chili con Carne #1

This dish can be served as a meaty entree, a stew, over rice or in a tortilla as a burrito. It can also be served with diced or baked potatoes. Alone, green chili con carne is nicely accompanied by rice, beans and hot corn tortillas.

1½ lb. BEEF CHUCK
GARLIC POWDER
SALT/PEPPER to taste
1 tsp. OIL (to brown meat)
4 Tbsp. OIL (to brown flour)
4 Tbsp. FLOUR
2 Tbsp. ONION, chopped
5 stewed TOMATOES, chopped
4 ANAHEIM CHILES, diced
¾ cup MEAT BROTH (meat juices)

Cut meat into bite-size pieces, season well before cooking. Heat skillet, add oil and brown meat, saving meat juices. Add water as needed to make meat broth (at least ¾ cup), cover. Once meat is cooked, set aside.

In a cooking pot, heat oil and brown flour. Add onion and saute, then add tomatoes, chiles and mix well. Add meat broth, stirring over low heat. Simmer 5 to 8 minutes, covered.

Add meat to cooking pot, mix, simmer for 10 minutes over low heat. Leave covered until serving time. (Serves 4 to 6)

Green Chili con Carne #2

2 tsp. OIL
3 cups cooked, lean GROUND BEEF
3 Tbsp. diced ONION
½ cup fresh TOMATOES, chopped
4-oz. can diced GREEN CHILES
½ tsp. SALT
½ tsp. coarsely-ground PEPPER
¼ tsp. GARLIC POWDER

In a cooking pot, heat oil, add meat and onion. Cook for a few minutes. Add tomatoes, green chiles and seasonings. Cover and simmer 10 minutes. (Serves 4 to 5)

Chili con Carne #1

Whether wrapped in a tortilla or served on a plate with rice and beans, chili con carne is a favorite Mexican dish.

1½ lbs. ROUND STEAK (cut in bite-size cubes)
2 Tbsp. SHORTENING
2 to 3 Tbsp. OIL
3 Tbsp. FLOUR
2 cups WATER (warm)
6 Tbsp. CHILI POWDER (with cumin)
1 tsp. SALT
¼ tsp. GARLIC POWDER

In a large skillet, brown meat cubes in shortening until well cooked. Push meat to one side of skillet and add oil and flour to make a quick gravy. Allow flour to cook for a few minutes, then mix with meat cubes. Stir and heat for five minutes. (Add ⅛ cup of water if meat becomes dry.) Leave covered, off heat, set aside.

To warm water, add chili powder and dissolve. (Make sure your chili powder has the seasoning cumin. This gives an added flavorful taste to chili con carne.) Add salt and garlic powder to chili mixture and stir. Then add chili to meat and mix thoroughly over medium heat. Heat to a boil, then reduce heat and let simmer, stirring frequently from 5 to 8 minutes. Remove from heat and leave covered until ready to serve. You should have a rich, gravy-like chili and meat. (Serves 6)

To serve: roll up chili con carne in a hot flour tortilla and serve with pinto beans or serve as a main dish.

Chili con Carne with Beans

1 lb. GROUND BEEF
4 Tbsp. FLOUR
1 tsp. SALT
4 Tbsp. CHILI POWDER
3 cups WATER
15-oz. can PINTO BEANS (or kidney beans, drained)
diced ONION and grated mild cheese for garnish

Brown meat and drain. Add flour, salt, chili powder and water. Bring to a boil. Add beans and blend in well. Simmer over low heat for 25 minutes. Garnish with onion and/or cheese, as desired. (Serves 4 to 6) Serve with cornbread sticks!

Burritos de Frijole y Carne
(Beef-Bean Burritos)

Here is a variation to the combination burros. Many dishes of the Southwest are a combination of Mexican and American influences. This recipe is an example!

  1 lb. lean GROUND BEEF, cooked, drained
  SALT to taste
  ¼ tsp. PAPRIKA
  ⅛ tsp. GARLIC SALT
  2 Tbsp. diced ONION
  1 Tbsp. diced GREEN PEPPER
  8-oz. can REFRIED BEANS
  6 FLOUR TORTILLAS (burro size)
  SALSA

In a skillet, heat cooked meat and season. Add onion and green pepper. Cook until green pepper is tender.

Heat refried beans. Use a small amount of water to make cooking easier.

Warm tortillas.

Combine beans and ground beef mixture. Cook until fully heated.

Place bean/meat mixture on tortillas and wrap into burros. Serve with salsa. (Makes 6)

Chili con Carne #2

Chili con carne with ground beef makes a delicious variation to "steak" Chili Con Carne!

  2 lbs. GROUND BEEF
  small chopped ONION
  minced GARLIC CLOVE
  ½ tsp. SALT/PEPPER if desired
  2 cups WATER
  3 Tbsp. CHILI POWDER
  4-oz. can TOMATO PASTE
  16-oz. can whole, peeled, STEWED TOMATOES

Brown meat, then drain. Cook meat with onions and minced garlic clove. Add salt and pepper. Cover and let simmer.

To water, dissolve chili powder and add to meat. Mix in tomato paste and stewed tomatoes. Stir thoroughly. Simmer for 2 hours, stirring occasionally until chili con carne is thick. (Serves 6 to 8)

Saucy Burritos

1½ lbs. GROUND BEEF
2 Tbsp. yellow ONION, diced
4-oz. can GREEN CHILES, chopped
1 tsp. SALT
¼ tsp. PEPPER
dash SWEET BASIL

Brown ground beef. Drain, then add onion, chiles and seasonings. Mix well, cook an extra 2 to 3 minutes. Leave aside, away from heat.

6-oz. can TOMATO SAUCE
½ cup WATER
2 Tbsp. TOMATO PASTE
2 pinches OREGANO
¼ tsp. SALT
PEPPER to taste
dash GARLIC SALT
2 tsp. CHILI POWDER

In a saucepan, blend tomato sauce, water, tomato paste, oregano, salt, pepper, garlic salt and chili powder. Mix in saucepan, heat to a boil, then simmer.

6 FLOUR TORTILLAS (12-inch)
SOUR CREAM, sliced BLACK OLIVES, Jack CHEESE

Take a flour tortilla and add 3 tablespoons of ground beef filling. Roll tortilla up snugly; fix rest of tortillas in the same way.

Pour tomato-chile sauce into a square baking dish. Place burritos side-by-side in the dish over the sauce. Pour remainder of sauce over burritos to cover them. Place in 350 F oven for 15 to 20 minutes.

Serve one burrito per plate. Line top of burrito with sour cream, olives and cheese. Serve with shredded lettuce at side of burrito, together with beans and rice. (Serves 6)

● **Garlic powder can be used as a substitute for garlic salt.**

Red Chili Burro #2

1½ lbs. ROUND STEAK (tenderized), cubed
1 Tbsp. SHORTENING
6 Tbsp. CHILI POWDER
2 cups WATER + ¼ cup MEAT JUICES from meat
2 to 3 Tbsp. OIL
3 Tbsp. FLOUR
1 tsp. SALT
¼ tsp. GARLIC SALT (or powder)
pinch OREGANO (ground)
2 crushed leaves of CILANTRO
6 FLOUR TORTILLAS

Cut meat into bite-size cubes, then brown in shortening. Save meat juices, ¼ cup or so should be left. Put meat aside. Dissolve chili powder in 2 cups of water and meat juices you saved. In a saucepan, heat oil and brown flour. Add chili mixture to this and bring to a slow boil. Stir often to keep from sticking or over-cooking. Add meat cubes, then blend in seasonings and spices. Mix thoroughly. Bring to a boil, then reduce heat, cover and simmer 10 minutes. Stir frequently.

Remove from heat. Leave covered until ready to use. Then, warm tortillas on both sides. Add chili/meat mixture in a row to one side of tortilla. Fold bottom end of tortilla up then roll tortilla over snugly. (Makes 6 burros)

Serve with salsa.

Arroz con Camaron (Rice and Shrimp)

1 cup WHITE RICE
4 Tbsp. SHORTENING
2 Tbsp. FLOUR
3 Tbsp. diced ONION
   ¼ tsp. PAPRIKA
   4 to 5 STEWED TOMATOES
   3 cups cooked, deveined SHRIMP

½ cup chopped CELERY
1 tsp. SALT
⅛ tsp. GARLIC POWDER
⅛ tsp. black PEPPER

Cook rice until tender.

In a skillet, add shortening and brown flour. Saute onion and celery when flour is brown. Then add seasonings. Add tomatoes, blend well.

Add rice next, cover and simmer for 15 minutes. Then add shrimp and cook over medium heat for 10 to 15 minutes until shrimp is fully heated. (Serves 6)

Shrimp Casserole

3 to 4 quarts WATER
2 tsp. OLIVE OIL
1 Tbsp. SALT
12 oz. EGG NOODLES
2 Tbsp. BUTTER
¼ tsp. PEPPER
3 Tbsp. PARSLEY FLAKES
1 can condensed CHEDDAR CHEESE SOUP (15 oz.)
1 cup HALF & HALF
½ cup WATER
1 cup cooked, sliced MUSHROOMS
2 cups soft BREAD CRUMBS
1 cup cooked PEAS (fresh, frozen or canned)
1 cup sliced BLACK OLIVES
2 cups cooked, shelled, deveined SHRIMP

In a cooking pot, bring water to a fast boil. Add olive oil, salt and noodles. Cook noodles until tender. Drain and place in large mixing bowl. Add butter evenly to noodles. Add pepper and parsley flakes and mix in well.

In a saucepan heat cheddar cheese soup. Add half & half and water. Blend until creamy and smooth. Add mushrooms and mix thoroughly. Cover and simmer for 10 minutes.

Add bread crumbs, peas and olives to soup mixture. Combine soup mixture with noodles. Add shrimp and blend evenly.

Preheat oven to 375 F. Butter large casserole dish and pour mixture in. Add cheese sauce over casserole and bake for 20-25 minutes until cheese sauce is bubbly. (Serves 6 to 8)

Cheese Sauce for Shrimp Casserole

1 cup BUTTERMILK (or evaporated milk)
1 Tbsp. CORN STARCH
¼ tsp. SALT
⅛ tsp. PEPPER
2 Tbsp. BUTTER
½ to 1 cup shredded CHEDDAR CHEESE

Heat buttermilk, add corn starch, blend in. Add salt, pepper and butter. Add cheese and heat until it melts. Sauce should have a creamy texture. Pour over casserole before baking.

Shrimp Saute

2 tsp. OLIVE OIL
2 cups cooked SHRIMP
6 to 8 CHERRY TOMATOES, sliced in half
½ cup PIMIENTOS, cut in strips
1 Tbsp. PARSLEY FLAKES
½ tsp. coarse ONION SALT
SALT/PEPPER to taste
dash GARLIC POWDER
1 Tbsp. LEMON JUICE
1 large, ripe AVOCADO, cut in thick strips

Heat oil and saute shrimp until fully heated. Add tomatoes and pimientos. Sprinkle in seasonings. Add lemon juice. Blend in well. Add avocado last. Cover, remove from heat and let sit for a few minutes. Then stir to redistribute flavor evenly. Serve immediately! (Serves 4)

Mexican Shrimp Creole

1 cup white long-grain RICE
1 Tbsp. OLIVE OIL
2 Tbsp. diced RED ONION
½ cup chopped GREEN PEPPER
2 Tbsp. FLOUR
1 Tbsp. PARSLEY
1 tsp. SALT
¼ tsp. PEPPER
2 tsp. CHILI POWDER
2 cups WATER
4 STEWED TOMATOES, chopped
1 cup CANNED PEAS, drained
1½ Tbsp. WHITE VINEGAR
½ cup RAISINS
3 cups cooked, shelled, deveined SHRIMP

Cook rice until tender. Drain and set aside. In a skillet, heat olive oil and saute onion. Add green pepper and flour. Cook until flour is browned. Add seasonings, parsley and chili powder, then add water slowly to avoid spattering.

Simmer, covered, 15 minutes. Add remaining ingredients. Cook 15 minutes more, covered, until shrimp is fully heated. (Serves 6)

Camaron Cocido (Shrimp Stew)

There is nothing like the meaty, savory taste of fresh shrimp sauted to a delicate glowing pink! Make this shrimp stew with your favorite vegetables.

2 lbs. fresh SHRIMP
STOCK from shrimp (about 4 cups)
2 Tbsp. OLIVE OIL
½ cup chopped CELERY
1 small GREEN PEPPER, chopped
1 bunch GREEN ONIONS, chopped
2/3 cup small MUSHROOMS, cooked
6 Tbsp. CHILI POWDER
1 to 2 CHILITEPINS (minced)
½ tsp. THYME
¼ tsp. PEPPER
¾ tsp. SALT
1 tsp. OREGANO
1 tsp. ground PARSLEY
½ tsp. GARLIC POWDER
2 large cooked SQUASH, sliced
½ cup BLACK OLIVES, sliced
6 to 8 pickled YELLOW PEPPERS

Wash shrimp and cook in salted water, covered. Cook until shells turn pink. Save all the stock from cooking. When shrimp is cooked, drain, shell and devein. Chop into bite-size pieces.

In a skillet, heat olive oil and saute celery, peppers, onion and mushrooms until fairly tender.

In a Dutch oven or cooking pot, add stock, chili powder and minced chilitepins. Dissolve chili powder and bring to a slow boil. Add seasonings and blend well. Add sauted vegetables and simmer 15 minutes covered. Stir in chopped shrimp and cook for 40 to 45 minutes over low heat, stirring occasionally. Add cooked squash and black olives during last 10 to 15 minutes of cooking time. Garnish with pickled yellow peppers. (Serves 6 to 8)

● **A couple of tablespoons of vinegar will take the "sting" out of "hot" chile salsas or chile dishes.**

Mexican Pepper Steak and Noodles

1½ lb. ROUND STEAK, tenderized
¼ cup MEAT JUICES
3 Tbsp. OIL
2 Tbsp. FLOUR
½ small ONION, diced
2 cooked GREEN CHILES, chopped
SALT/PEPPER/GARLIC POWDER
dash OREGANO
6 oz. EGG NOODLES

Cut steak into cubes, brown in skillet. Save meat juices. Place meat aside. Heat oil and brown flour. Cook onion. Add chiles and cook for a few minutes. Blend in meat juices and 2/3 cup water, mix well. Add meat cubes and seasonings, cover, simmer over reduced heat for 20 minutes.

Cook noodles in 3 quarts boiling water with 2 teaspoons salt and ½ teaspoon oil. Drain noodles and butter lightly. Combine noodles with steak mixture, simmer 10 minutes. Serve hot. (Makes 4 to 5 servings)

Chile-Cheese Casserole

½ cup EVAPORATED MILK
½ cup soft BREAD CRUMBS
2 Tbsp. BUTTER
2 cups elbow MACARONI (cooked)
1 cup shredded cheddar CHEESE
¼ cup minced PARSLEY
1 tsp. SALT
⅛ tsp. PEPPER
⅛ tsp. SWEET BASIL
4-oz. can chopped GREEN CHILES

In a large saucepan, add milk and heat to a fast boil. Reduce heat and sprinkle in bread crumbs, then add butter, mix and allow butter to melt.

In a mixing bowl, place macaroni, drained and hot, and add cheese. Then, add all seasonings, mix well. Take milk mixture and add to bowl, blend well. Add chiles and mix.

Place in a greased casserole dish. Bake at 350 F for 25 to 30 minutes until cheese is bubbly. (Serves 6)

Chimichangas

Chimichangas are flour tortillas stuffed with meat, beans, cheese, etc., deep-fried to a golden brown and garnished with lettuce, tomato, cheese or hot salsa.

¼ cup OIL
8 Tbsp. FLOUR
1 medium ONION, diced
5 large chopped STEWED TOMATOES
2 lbs. cooked CHUCK ROAST (cut into bite-size)
2 cups BEEF STOCK (saved from pot-cooked meat)
8 medium diced ANAHEIM CHILES
    (canned or roasted)
SALT/PEPPER to taste
1 tsp. GARLIC POWDER
5 to 7 cups WATER
8 to 10 large FLOUR TORTILLAS

In cooking pot, heat oil and brown flour. Add onion and stewed tomatoes and cook 2 minutes. Add meat, then add 2 cups beef stock. Heat over medium heat, stirring frequently. Add diced chiles, salt, pepper, garlic powder. Add water and mix. Heat at high heat, uncovered, for 15 minutes, stirring frequently until mixture is thickened. Remove to low heat. Simmer until ready to use.

Add ½ cup meat mixture to a heated flour tortilla. Place filling at one end of tortilla, then fold tortilla as follows: fold bottom edge over filling, then fold both sides to the center. Roll the side with the meat filling all the way over and form a burrito. Deep fry chimichanga to a golden brown but do not over-fry. Make 2 to 3 chimichangas at a time. Use tongs to place and remove chimichangas from hot oil. Place chimichangas on their "seam" to seal. This makes them easier to turn. (Makes 8 to 10)

● **Use VERY HOT OIL when frying, to cook foods faster and to prevent foods from becoming saturated.**

Chimichangas de Frijoles y Queso

1 to 2 Tbsp. OIL
2 cans (16 oz.) REFRIED BEANS
1½ cups grated LONGHORN CHEESE
8 to 10 FLOUR TORTILLAS
OIL for deep frying
shredded LETTUCE
TACO SALSA (see Salsa Section)
shredded CHEESE

In a large skillet, heat oil. Spoon in beans and a small amount of water as needed to make beans easier to cook. Cover over medium heat, stirring frequently until well heated. Blend in cheese. Mix thoroughly. Beans should be fairly thick to make a good filling for chimichangas. Cook beans until cheese is melted. Remove from heat and leave nearby.

Take 3 or 4 flour tortillas and add to each ½ cup of beans and cheese (approximately), to one end of tortilla. Then fold bottom and top edges over to cover part of filling. Fold over at end where filling is and roll over as you would a burrito, but in this case tuck both ends in. Then heat oil in a fry pan and fry chimichangas.

Use either a pan or deep fryer with cooking tongs if you have them. If you do use a fry pan, place chimichangas in the hot oil at the seam so it is sealed first. This way the filling will stay in place. Work with chimichangas one at a time but fry up to four when using a fry pan.

Fry until golden brown. Place in lined bowl, then garnish each with lettuce, salsa and cheese. (Makes 8 to 10 Bean and Cheese Chimichangas!)

Mexican Meat Loaf

1½ lbs. GROUND BEEF
1 well-beaten EGG
1 cup dry BREAD CRUMBS
16-oz. can STEWED TOMATOES
4-oz. can GREEN CHILES
2 Tbsp. finely-diced ONION

1¼ tsp. SALT
¼ tsp. GARLIC SALT
¼ tsp. OREGANO
⅛ tsp. PAPRIKA
PARSLEY FLAKES

In a large bowl, mix meat and egg, add bread crumbs. Mix tomatoes, green chiles, onion and add to meat mixture. Blend in seasonings and combine thoroughly.

Make into a loaf and put in a lightly-greased loaf pan, 9x5x3. Bake at 375 F for one hour. Garnish with parsley flakes. (Serves 6)

Carne Asada (Roast Beef)

In the Southwest, broiled meat is often accompanied by a tasty chili salsa or chili mixture. Serve with corn tortillas, whole pinto beans or refried beans.

2½ lbs. ROUND STEAK, tenderized
⅛ tsp. SALT/PEPPER
⅛ tsp. GARLIC POWDER (or garlic salt)
2 tsp. OLIVE OIL
½ small ONION, chopped
¼ cup RAISINS
2 medium-sized TOMATOES, peeled, chopped
3 JALAPEÑO CHILES, cut in lengthwise strips
¼ tsp. THYME
1 tsp. VINEGAR

Make slits in the steak and season with salt, pepper, and garlic powder or salt. Broil in outdoor grill or oven broiler. Cook as desired.

In a saucepan, heat olive oil and saute onions. Add raisins, tomatoes and chiles. Season, then add vinegar and cook over high heat, then reduce heat to simmer. Cover. Simmer for 5 to 8 minutes.

When meat is cooked, serve with chili mixture. (Serves 6)

Stuffed Peppers

1½ lbs. GROUND BEEF
3 large stewed TOMATOES, chopped
½ tsp. GARLIC SALT
¾ tsp. SALT
½ tsp. coarsely-ground PEPPER
⅛ tsp. ground THYME
2 diced JALAPEÑO CHILES
¼ cup long-grain white RICE
10 GREEN PEPPERS (uncooked)
1½ cups WATER
6 oz. TOMATO SAUCE

Place meat in a large mixing bowl. Then, in a smaller bowl combine tomatoes and all seasonings. Mix well. Add this to meat and blend in jalapeños using your hands. Cook rice, drain and blend into meat mixture.

Take each green pepper and pack with meat/rice mixture. Then place in Dutch oven. Add water and tomato sauce. Bring to a boil, uncovered. Then cover, reduce heat to medium, and cook for 50 minutes, until green peppers are tender and meat is fully cooked. (Makes 10 stuffed peppers)

Mexi-Burgers

Turn your hamburger cook-out into a Mexican fiesta!

1½ lbs. GROUND BEEF
3 Tbsp. chopped ONIONS
3 Tbsp. diced GREEN CHILES
1 tsp. SALT
¼ tsp. GARLIC SALT
¼ tsp. BLACK PEPPER
⅛ tsp. PAPRIKA

Take meat and mix in onions, green chiles and seasonings. Form into 6 patties. Fry over medium heat. Serve on warm buns. (Serves 6)

Salsa for Hamburgers

6-oz. can TOMATO SAUCE
2 Tbsp. TOMATO PASTE
½ tsp. SALT
¼ tsp. GARLIC POWDER
¼ tsp. BLACK PEPPER

Mix all ingredients in saucepan. Add small amount of water as needed. Heat til bubbly.

Pour some sauce in skillet, place cooked hamburgers in skillet and add remainder of sauce. Cover, heat for 2 to 3 minutes. Serve burgers hot with sauce over them!

Guacamole Burgers

6 hefty HAMBURGER patties, cooked as desired
6 RED ONION rings
6 FRENCH ROLLS, warmed
6 leaves ROMAINE LETTUCE

Cook meat patties as desired, drain.

Warm rolls, add lettuce, cooked meat patties and 3 to 4 tablespoons of **Guacamole**. Top with red onion rings. Serve at once. (Serves 6) Serve with a side dish of fresh pinto beans!

Guacamole

1 large AVOCADO, mashed
⅛ tsp. SALT
½ Tbsp. LIME JUICE
½ tsp. TABASCO SAUCE
1 small, peeled, chopped TOMATO
½ tsp. DRY MUSTARD

In bowl, combine all ingredients, blend well until smooth and creamy.

Quesadillas

Quesadillas make a satisfying meal. Serve with hot salsa, rice and beans!

1½ cups MASA HARINA
¾ cup WATER (more if necessary)
1 well-beaten EGG
small can GREEN CHILES, cut in strips
4 oz. CHEESE, cut in strips

Mix masa harina and water, add egg. Knead to form 12 dough balls. Place in large bowl, cover to keep moist. Using rolling pin, flatten out dough balls to form circles. Place dough over waxed paper to keep from sticking. Then place cheese strips and chili strips at center of circle. Fold dough over to form a half-circle. Press edges with fork to seal.

Using fork, make small indentations over top of quesadillas. Then fry in a deep skillet until golden brown. Be sure to fry both sides of quesadillas. Garnish with hot salsa. (Makes 12, serve two per plate)

Carne Seca

Carne seca means "dry meat." Brisket is often used, since it has less meat juices than other cuts of meat. Carne seca (or carne machaca) is stew-cooked and separated into strings of meat. It is used in burros, chimichangas, tacos and when blended with green chile, onion and stewed tomatoes makes a delicious green chili con carne!

To make **Carne Seca Stew**, cook 1½ to 2 pounds of brisket in a Dutch oven. Season meat, cover and cook over medium heat with a small amount of water. Cook meat until fully cooked. When meat has cooked thoroughly, allow to cool down, then separate into pieces and cut into bite-size strings of meat.

Carne Seca Burros

   2 tsp. OLIVE OIL
   ½ small diced ONION
   4-oz. can GREEN CHILES, diced
   4 stewed TOMATOES
   SALT/PEPPER to taste
   ¼ tsp. GARLIC POWDER
   1½ to 2 lbs. cooked CARNE SECA (cut in pieces)
   6 FLOUR TORTILLAS

In a skillet, heat oil and saute onion, green chiles and tomatoes. Add seasonings and blend in meat. Cook, covered for 10 minutes. Then cook an additional 15 minutes uncovered, stirring frequently. Keep meat mixture dry. Warm tortillas and add meat. Roll up into burros. Serves 6)

Carne Seca Tacos

Fix meat as you would for **Carne Seca Burros** and add to warmed, ready-made taco shells. (1½ to 2 pounds brisket yields approximately enough meat for 12 to 14 tacos). Garnish with lettuce, taco salsa, grated cheese.

Chile Relleno (Stuffed Chiles)

Chiles are stuffed, then dipped in an egg batter and fried or baked to a golden brown. They can be stuffed with meats, picadillo (minced meat), corn and cheeses.

8 GREEN CHILES, long and straight
8 strips MONTEREY JACK CHEESE
FLOUR for dusting chiles
6 EGGS, separated
½ tsp. SALT
pinch BAKING POWDER
1 Tbsp. MILK (or evaporated milk)
OIL for frying chiles

Roast chiles in oven 350 F for 10 minutes, until skin is easily removed (or roast over top burner). Take roasted chiles and place in a wet paper towel or kitchen towel and leave there a few minutes. Skin is easier to remove by this method.

Remove skins, then rinse in cold water and paper towel dry. Make a small slit at base of stem and remove seeds, but leave stem intact. Insert a strip of cheese in chiles and try not to tear chiles. Dust chiles in flour evenly and leave on plate nearby.

In a bowl, beat egg whites with salt and baking powder. Beat until egg whites are stiff.

In a separate bowl, slightly beat egg yolks with milk. Add egg yolks to egg whites and stir bowl with hands gently, twice.

Heat oil in fry pan or deep fryer. Then dip floured chiles in egg batter and fry until golden brown. Drain lightly, then serve immediately. (Makes 8)

Chile Relleno con Queso

8 GREEN CHILES, cooked
8 strips CHEESE (longhorn, cheddar, jack)
6 EGGS, separated
4 Tbsp. FLOUR
1 Tbsp. WATER
¼ tsp. SALT
¼ tsp. BAKING POWDER
dash BLACK PEPPER

Roast chiles in 350 F oven for 10 minutes, until chile skin is easily removed. Chiles should be tender-firm. Peel skin and remove stem and seedy part under stem. Insert cheese strips in chiles. Try not to tear chile.

In a bowl, beat egg whites until stiff. In another bowl whip yolks, add flour, water, salt, baking powder and pepper. Blend and mix with egg whites.

Dust stuffed chiles with flour. Then butter a square baking pan. Place floured chiles in pan side by side, then pour egg misture over them. Put in 350 F oven for 10 to 15 minutes until egg is golden brown.

Serve 2 chile rellenos per plate. Chili sauce or salsa may be used over rellenos.

Menu Suggestion:

- Chile relleno con queso
- Tamale
- Refried beans
- Rice

Mexican Steak and Rice

2 lbs. ROUND STEAK (tenderized)
1 to 2 tsp. OIL
2 minced GARLIC CLOVES
½ cup WATER

Cut meat into cubes. In a skillet, heat oil and saute garlic cloves. Add meat cubes and water. Cover and brown meat over reduced heat. When meat is cooked, drain meat juices and save. Place meat in a bowl and put aside.

3 Tbsp. OIL (salad, olive or safflower)
½ lb. long-grain RICE
½ small ONION, diced
2/3 cup MEAT JUICES (saved from cooking steak)
2 cups HOT WATER
½ tsp. PEPPER
1 Tbsp. SALT
¼ cup crushed CILANTRO
6 oz. TOMATO SAUCE
2 oz. TOMATO PUREE

In the same skillet, heat oil, add rice and brown over medium heat, stirring constantly. Add onion and saute briskly. Blend in meat juices and add water. Add remaining ingredients. Mix well. Add meat, cover and cook over medium heat for 40 to 45 minutes. Stir occasionally to keep rice from sticking. Cook until rice is tender. (Serves 6 to 8)

Chile Relleno de Maiz

8 large CHILES (ancho or Anaheim)
15-oz. can cream-style CORN
1 cup shredded LONGHORN CHEESE
½ cup chopped PIMIENTO
¼ cup diced ONION
2 EGGS
½ cup MILK
2 Tbsp. FLOUR
dash SALT
pinch BAKING POWDER
OIL for frying

If you use fresh chiles, roast or deep fry to remove skin. Make a slit big enough to remove seeds and allow for filling. Remove seeds but leave stem in place.

In a bowl, combine corn, cheese, pimiento and onion. Cook over medium heat until fairly thickened. Cool.

Combine eggs, milk, flour, salt and baking powder in a mixing bowl and beat until batter is creamy.

Stuff chiles with cooled corn filling, being careful not to tear chile. Squeeze chile a little to seal filling. In a heavy skillet or deep fryer, heat enough oil to fry chiles.

Dip each filled chile in batter, then fry until golden brown. Keep in a warmer until all chiles are done. Do 2 to 3 chiles at a time. When all chiles are fried, make chili sauce. (Makes 8)

Chili Sauce for Rellenos

3 Tbsp. OIL
3 Tbsp. FLOUR
2 cups WATER
6 Tbsp. CHILI POWDER
¼ tsp. GARLIC SALT
SALT to taste
½ cup TOMATO PUREE
⅛ tsp. ground CUMIN

In a saucepan, heat oil and brown flour. Dissolve chili powder in water, then mix with browned flour. Add seasonings and tomato puree. Cook to a boil, reduce heat and simmer until thickened.

Pour chili sauce over chile rellenos and serve.

Cabbage Rolls

There are two methods to prepare them, in a Dutch oven or a crockpot.

1 large GREEN CABBAGE
½ cup cooked and drained WHITE RICE
1½ lbs. lean GROUND BEEF
1 can whole STEWED TOMATOES, chopped
1 medium ONION, chopped
PEPPER/SALT/GARLIC POWDER to taste
2 finely-chopped JALAPEÑOS

Parboil cabbage until leaves are easily removed from stem. Cabbage should be firmly tender so that it isn't overcooked. Parboil rice in small saucepan but don't overcook.

Brown meat and drain. Mix meat with rice, onion, 1 cup of tomatoes, the spices and finely-chopped jalapeños. Mix thoroughly.

In Dutch oven, place rest of tomatoes. Add enough water to make the Dutch oven 1/3 full. Bring to a boil then reduce heat to medium.

Take 1 cabbage leaf and put ½ cup meat mixture at stem of leaf. Roll leaf so it completely envelops meat. Place in Dutch oven, cook at medium heat for 45 minutes until cabbage is fully cooked. (Serves 6 to 8)

Crockpot Method

Fix meat same as above. Take 12 cabbage leaves and place in hot water to blanch. Then add meat to leaves as above. Cook in crockpot at low heat for 6 to 8 hours or at high heat for 3 to 4 hours.

● **Mix hot chiles with milder chiles, or use fewer of the hot chiles, since their flavor will go a long way.**

Chalupas

Chalupas are fried corn or flour tortillas which cup a meat mixture, refried beans or guacamole, and are garnished with lettuce, olives, cheese, topped by dressing.

½ cup VEGETABLE OIL (for frying)
8 CORN TORTILLAS
½ small coarsely-chopped ONION
3 chopped STEWED TOMATOES
15-oz. can ROAST BEEF
SALT/PEPPER/GARLIC POWDER to taste
4-oz. can chopped GREEN CHILES (drained)
shredded LETTUCE for garnish
1 cup grated CHEESE
AVOCADO DRESSING

Heat oil in a frypan. Using tongs, dip a corn tortilla in the hot oil on one side. Quickly turn tortilla around, pressing down and frying each of three sides. Fry the side held by the tongs until all sides of the tortilla are raised. Fry center of tortilla by placing it in hot oil and holding it down by using tongs. Remove from pan, drain on paper towels. Do the remaining tortillas in this fashion.

In a saucepan, heat a little oil and saute onion. Add tomatoes and roast beef. Cook 2 minutes, mix well. Season as desired. Fill each chalupa with roast beef mixture, green chiles. Top with lettuce, sprinkle with cheese, and add Avocado Dressing over each. (Makes 8 chalupas)

Avocado Dressing for Chalupas

1 cup mashed AVOCADO
2 Tbsp. LEMON JUICE
3 Tbsp. EVAPORATED MILK
1 Tbsp. CREAM CHEESE
½ tsp. SALT
⅛ tsp. OREGANO
dash GARLIC SALT
1 tsp. DRY MUSTARD
1 Tbsp. minced PIMIENTO

In a bowl, mash avocado and mix in all ingredients. Blend well, use blender at lowest speed. Dressing should be fairly thick. If too thick, add small amount of milk. (Makes 1¼ cups)

Bebidas/Beverages

Champurro (Mexican Cocoa)

Champurro is a rich, creamy cocoa drink, traditionally a wedding drink. It is served hot and can be topped with whipped cream.

1 cup EVAPORATED MILK
1 cup WATER
3 Tbsp. FLOUR
4 Tbsp. COCOA
dash SALT
8 tsp. SUGAR

Heat milk and water to a fast boil, stirring frequently. Reduce heat.

In a mixing bowl, mix flour, cocoa, salt and sugar with ¼ cup water. Blend until smooth and creamy. Add cocoa mixture to milk mixture and blend in well. Cook over medium heat, stirring constantly until thick. Allow Champurro to come to a carefully watched bubbly boil. Serve in mugs. Sprinkle with a dash of nutmeg. (Makes 2 cups)

Tamarindo

Tamarindo is the fruit of a tree by the same name. Tamarindo is used for making preservatives, flavoring beverages and can be eaten fresh. In our house it is taken as a "health" drink. It can be sweetened with honey and is always served chilled!

1¾ quarts WATER
3 or 4 TAMARINDOS
1/3 cup BROWN SUGAR
1 tsp. ground CINNAMON

Bring water to a boil in a two-quart pot. Wash and peel shell from tamarindos. Cook over medium heat until tamarindos are tender. Remove tamarindos and strain extract. Pour extract into a container, add sugar and cinnamon (add honey, if desired). Blend well. Chill and serve with ice. (Serves 4 to 5)

Leche de Chocolate (Chocolate Milk)

1 oz. UNSWEETENED CHOCOLATE
½ cup boiling WATER
2/3 cup BROWN SUGAR
8 cups MILK
dash SALT
½ tsp. VANILLA
⅛ tsp. ground CINNAMON

Melt chocolate then blend in boiling water. Add sugar and dissolve thoroughly. Add salt and milk, bring to a slow boil. Reduce heat and stir in vanilla and cinnamon. Serve in mugs, topped with whipped cream if desired. (Serves 6)

Leche con Anís (Flavored Milk)

I've always enjoyed the licorice-like taste of anise, so I enjoyed drinking leche con anise! Serve it hot or cold for a nutritious snack.

4 cups MILK
2 Tbsp. BROWN SUGAR (2/3 Tbsp. Piloncillo)
1 level tsp. ground ANISE
4 CINNAMON sticks

Heat milk and dissolve brown sugar. Add anise and blend in well. Serve piping hot or cold with cinnamon sticks.

Anise and hot chocolate is also very tasty. Use regular pre-sweetened chocolate, add anise and serve hot with whipped cream and cinnamon sticks!

Pinole (Corn Drink)

Pinole is roasted ground corn. It makes a delightful and nutritious breakfast drink. If made with more milk and warmed, it can be a hot breakfast cereal.

½ cup or so of PINOLE
MILK (or water)
SUGAR

In a glass, add 6 to 8 tablespoons of pinole. Add milk or water to make a glassful. Sweeten with brown or white sugar, mix well and drink cold or warm.

Fiesta Egg Nog

1½ cups EVAPORATED MILK
2/3 cup WATER
2 well-beaten EGGS
2 Tbsp. FLOUR
2 Tbsp. SUGAR
dash SALT
dash NUTMEG
3 oz. LIGHT RUM
½ tsp. VANILLA

In a saucepan, heat milk and water, bring to a fast boil, then remove from heat.

In a mixing bowl, combine eggs, flour, salt, nutmeg, sugar and ¼ cup water. Whip to a creamy texture. (Add a little more water if necessary)

Combine egg mixture and milk mixture, blend well, cool slightly, then add rum and vanilla. Serve in mugs or tall chilled glasses. (Makes 2 servings)

Coffee Liqueur

3 cups WATER
10 tsp. (heaping) INSTANT COFFEE granules*
2 cups dark BROWN SUGAR (packed)
½ cup GRANULATED SUGAR
5 tsp. VANILLA EXTRACT
2 cups BRANDY

In a cooking pot, add water and dissolve coffee. Add sugars, blend well. Bring to a boil, reduce heat and simmer covered for 50 minutes. Stir every 15 minutes. Keep heat just under medium. Do not allow coffee mixture to overcook. Cook an extra 8 minutes at high flame stirring constantly to evaporate water from mixture a bit.

Mixture should be slightly thickened. Pour into a glass container without lid and cool.

When mixture is warm, but not hot, add vanilla, mix in gently. Add brandy, stir. Store in glass container with lid in dark place and use the next day. (Makes 24 ounces of coffee liqueur)

*Mexican coffee is characteristically richer and more full-bodied than many American coffees. Try Mexican Nescafé for superb-tasting coffee liqueur!

Café Mejicano (Mexican Coffee)

This recipe for Mexican Coffee is a strong remedy for those cold winter nights or a lonely heart!

1 cup hot COFFEE
1 oz. COFFEE LIQUEUR (Kahlúa)
½ oz. BRANDY
1 tsp. HONEY
dash CLOVES
WHIPPED CREAM

Use an over-sized coffee mug. Combine all ingredients in the order given. Top with whipped cream. (Serves 1)

Café Rico

1 cup hot COFFEE
1 oz. COFFEE LIQUEUR
3 Tbsp. EVAPORATED MILK
1 tsp. light BROWN SUGAR
dash CINNAMON
WHIPPED CREAM (or marshmallow cream)

Use an over-sized coffee mug. Combine all ingredients in the order given. Top with whipped cream or marshmallow cream. (Serves 1)

Café Helado de Almendra (Iced Coffee)

2 cups cold COFFEE
3 oz. AMARETTO
1 tsp. ground CINNAMON
1 cup CRUSHED ICE
8 oz. VANILLA ICE CREAM
WHIPPED CREAM
2 CHERRIES

Mix all ingredients except for the whipped cream and cherries in a blender. Blend well. Pour into 2 tall glasses. Top with whipped cream and cherries. (Serves 2)

Café de Almendra (Almond Coffee)

1 cup hot COFFEE
1½ oz. AMARETTO
4 oz. VANILLA ICE CREAM
WHIPPED TOPPING
CINNAMON

Use an over-sized coffee mug. Combine coffee and amaretto. Blend well. Spoon in ice cream, top with whipped topping and sprinkle with cinnamon. (Serves 1)

Café de Nieve (Ice Cream Coffee)

1 cup hot COFFEE
1½ oz. KAHLUA
½ pint ICE CREAM*
dash of NUTMEG
WHIPPED TOPPING

Use an over-sized mug. Combine coffee, Kahlúa, ice cream and nutmeg. Blend well. Top with whipped topping, and sprinkle with diced pecans. (Serves 1)

Strawberry Daiquiri

2 cups crushed ICE
8 oz. LIGHT RUM
3 oz. LIME JUICE
2 to 3 Tbsp. SUGAR
10-oz. pkg. frozen, thawed STRAWBERRIES in syrup
½ cup fresh, chopped STRAWBERRIES

Put ingredients in blender, mix well. Serve in chilled daiquiri glasses.
Top daiquiri with whipped cream for a tantalizing treat!
(Serves 6)

Kahlúa Naranjado

2 parts KAHLUA
1 part ORANGE JUICE

Mix well, pour in chilled glass or serve hot in a mug! (Makes 1 serving)

Tequila

Tequila is the national drink of Mexico. It is made from the fermented sap of the maguey plant which is a species of agave. There are four common forms of tequila: pulque, mescal, white or silver tequila and gold tequila.

Pulque is a coarse form of tequila. It has a sour taste and cloudy appearance. Mescal is a distilled form of pulque. White or silver tequila is distilled twice. It is colorless and odorless. Gold tequila is distilled and aged. It can be taken straight and is considered tequila at its best!

Since tequila is most often sold without aging it is best used for mixed drinks. One of the most popular drinks to complement Mexican dishes is the Margarita!

Margarita

COARSE SALT (kosher)
½ oz. LIME JUICE
1½ oz. TEQUILA
½ oz. TRIPLE SEC
crushed ICE

Moisten rim of glass and dip in salt. Combine lime juice, tequila, triple sec and crushed ice in a blender. Mix and pour into a glass!

Strawberry Margaritas for six

COARSE SALT (kosher)
10 oz. TEQUILA
4 oz. TRIPLE SEC
3 oz. LIME JUICE
10-oz. pkg. frozen, thawed STRAWBERRIES in syrup
crushed ICE

Moisten rim of six glasses and dip in salt. Chill. Combine all ingredients in a blender and mix. Pour into glasses and serve!

Margarita de Fresas

COARSE SALT (kosher)
2 oz. TEQUILA
¾ oz. TRIPLE SEC
½ oz. LIME JUICE
2 to 3 tsp. LIGHT CORN SYRUP
3 to 4 chopped STRAWBERRIES

Moisten rim of glass and dip in salt. Combine all ingredients in a blender and mix thoroughly. Pass through sieve once, then pour in blender with crushed ice and mix.
Pour into glass and enjoy!

Tequila Sunrise

1½ oz. TEQUILA
¾ oz. fresh ORANGE JUICE
½ oz. GRENADINE
MARASCHINO CHERRY

Mix tequila, orange juice, grenadine in a blender. Pour into a chilled glass, add cherry.

Bebida de Jengibre (Ginger Drink)

Southwest summers tend to be hot and this ginger-ade really quenches your thirst! For those cold winter days and nights, serve it hot!

1 medium-size GINGER ROOT
3 or 4 LEMONS
CINNAMON sticks

Take ginger root and wash well. Steep it for two hours in approximately 2 quarts of water. Remove root and pour ginger extract into container. You may want to pour extract through a sieve first. Squeeze lemons into the container and mix well. Stir. Chill. Serve with cinnamon sticks. (Makes 1 quart)
For hot ginger-ade, serve in mugs and sprinkle with a little nutmeg. Stir and serve with a cinnamon stick!

Postres/Desserts

Buñuelos (Fritters)

Buñuelos are quick-fried fritters topped by a brown sugar syrup. They are round, thin and crispy!

2 cups FLOUR
¾ tsp. SALT

4 Tbsp. SHORTENING
2/3 cup WATER

Combine flour and salt. Mix in shortening. Add water a little at a time to make a soft dough. Knead for 5 minutes and form 9 dough balls. On a lightly-floured cutting board, with a rolling pin, roll out round, thin sheets of dough as you would for tortillas. Quick-fry in hot oil, drain, then top with syrup. (Makes 9 buñuelos)

Miel (Syrup) for Buñuelos

2 cups light BROWN SUGAR
2 cups WATER
1 to 2 CINNAMON STICKS

In a saucepan, dissolve sugar in water evenly. Bring to a fast boil, then reduce heat. Stir frequently. Remove cover and cook over medium heat for 15 minutes more until thickened. Pour into serving container with cinnamon sticks. Leave sticks in syrup for 10 to 15 minutes, remove sticks before serving.

Mexican Wedding Cookies

These cookies are scrumptious, the kind you can't stop eating! If you are planning a wedding consider them as part of your food list.

1 cup softened BUTTER
1 tsp. VANILLA
½ cup confectioners SUGAR
2 cups FLOUR
¼ tsp. SALT
1 cup finely chopped PECANS

Cream butter, add vanilla. Stir to a light and fluffy texture. Add sugar and cream the mixture.

Mix flour and salt, and add creamed mixture. Sprinkle with pecans. Blend well. Form into 24 balls and flatten out lightly.

Bake at 350 F for 25 minutes or until lightly brown. (Makes 2 dozen cookies)

Biscochuelos (Honey Bread)

Biscochuelos is a Mexican sweet bread. It makes an excellent after-dinner dessert with coffee. Sliced and served with honey, butter or cream cheese, it makes a tasty snack!

3 cups FLOUR
1½ Tbsp. BAKING POWDER
1 tsp. SALT
1½ tsp. ground ANISE
1½ tsp. ground NUTMEG
1 tsp. CINNAMON
1 cup SUGAR + 2 Tbsp. BROWN SUGAR
1½ cups SHORTENING
2 Tbsp. HONEY

Mix flour, baking powder, salt, anise, nutmeg and cinnamon in large bowl, blend well. Cream sugars in shortening and add honey. Mix thoroughly, then add to dry ingredients. Make an elastic dough, knead and use small amounts of warm water to keep dough from sticking. Form a loaf and place in a well-greased loaf pan. Bake at 350 F for 45 minutes or until bread is brown. Insert a bread knife in the middle of the loaf to check if it is done. Make 5 more "holes" in the bread and add butter in holes. (Makes one loaf)

Arroz Dulce (Rice Pudding)

For a light dessert or snack, arroz dulce is a good choice. After a big meal this dessert is always welcomed.

2 cups cooked white, long grain RICE
1½ cups EVAPORATED MILK
½ cup RAISINS
½ cup SUGAR
½ tsp. VANILLA
dash NUTMEG
½ cup MILK

In a saucepan, mix rice and evaporated milk. Add raisins, sugar, vanilla, nutmeg. Blend thoroughly, then add ½ cup milk. Stir over medium heat until rice becomes thickened. Serve warm or chill in refrigerator for 30 minutes. Sprinkle with sugar crystals. (Serves 4-5)

Banana Spice Cake

This cake is delicious alone with coffee or tea, frosted, iced or topped with whipped cream! The original recipe calls for Piloncillo, Mexican brown sugar. It's sweeter and tastier than regular brown sugar. If you have the opportunity to use Piloncillo, then try it with this recipe!

2 Tbsp. BUTTER (or margarine)
2 cups light BROWN SUGAR (or 2/3 cup Piloncillo)
2 large overripe BANANAS, creamed
2 well-beaten EGGS
½ tsp. VANILLA
¼ cup SHORTENING
¼ cup granulated SUGAR
½ tsp. SALT
1½ cups CAKE FLOUR
3 tsp. BAKING POWDER
½ tsp. ground ANISE
½ tsp. ground CINNAMON
2/3 cup EVAPORATED MILK + 2 Tbsp. WATER
ground PECANS (optional)

In a saucepan melt butter and dissolve brown sugar. Add creamed bananas, mix well. Leave aside to cool.

Combine eggs and vanilla in a mixing bowl. Cream shortening and granulated sugar and add to egg mixture. Take cooled banana mixture and add to egg mixture. Mix thoroughly until creamy and smooth.

Mix salt, flour, baking powder, anise and cinnamon. Add milk to dry ingredients a little at a time, mixing as you add. Beat vigorously until smooth. Add water and mix. Pour cake batter into a well-greased and floured 9-inch cake pan. Spoon the banana mixture on the cake batter in a circular pattern evenly over batter.

Add ground pecans over batter, if desired. Bake at 350 F for 50 minutes until cake is golden brown and it separates a little around the side of the pan. (Makes one 9-inch cake)

Anise/Pecan Cookies

A good Mexican cook always keeps anise handy on the spice rack. These anise/pecan cookies are delicious with coffee or tea!

2¾ cups FLOUR
2 Tbsp. CORNSTARCH
½ tsp. SALT
2/3 cup softened MARGARINE (or butter)
½ cup SHORTENING   1/3 cup diced PECANS
½ cup LIGHT BROWN SUGAR   ½ pkg. dry active YEAST
½ tsp. crushed ANISE SEED   ½ cup warm WATER

In a bowl, combine flour, cornstarch and salt. Cream butter and shortening, add sugar. Mix in with flour mixture, add anise and pecans.

Dissolve yeast in warm water evenly. Preheat oven to 350 F. Blend in dissolved yeast to flour mixture to make a soft dough. Form dough into a roll and cut in half. Cut 12 cookies from each roll. Round cookies out and flatten a bit. Bake for 20 to 25 minutes. (Makes 2 dozen)

Chimichangas de Manzana
(Apple Fritters)

Fruit chimichangas are a Sunday morning delight! These apple chimichangas can be served any time and are quite easily made!

16-oz. can unsweetened APPLE PIE FILLING
6 Tbsp. CORN STARCH
½ cup SUGAR
1/3 cup BROWN SUGAR
1 tsp. ground CINNAMON
6 (12-inch) FLOUR TORTILLAS
OIL for frying

In a saucepan, heat and thicken apple filling with corn starch. Add white and brown sugar and cinnamon. When mixture thickens, leave covered to simmer for a few minutes. Taste for desired sweetness.

Take a flour tortilla and spoon on a row of apple mixture at one end of the tortilla. Fold over bottom, covering apple mixture, then fold over both sides. Roll tortilla up snugly. Prepare rest of tortillas in the same way.

Deep fry chimichangas to a golden brown. (Makes 6 fruit chimichangas) Use your favorite filling!

Mexican Christmas Cookies

With a set of cookie cutters you can make works of art with these cookies! Cookie making puts you in a festive mood. These cookies are good any time, any occasion!

    1 cup SHORTENING
    1¼ cups SUGAR
    1 EGG, beaten
    1/3 cup WARM MILK
    3¾ cups FLOUR
    ¼ tsp. SALT
    1 tsp. ALMOND EXTRACT
    ½ tsp. GROUND CLOVES
    1 tsp. CINNAMON
    ½ cup finely-chopped PECANS
    red and green DECORATING CRYSTALS

Cream shortening and sugar. Add egg and milk. Mix flour, salt and spices. Add pecans. Form into a dough, cover and chill for 2 hours. Knead dough, sprinkle with a little flour to keep from sticking. Cut dough into desired shapes, using cookie cutters. Place on lightly-greased cookie sheet. Bake at 375 F for 8 to 10 minutes or until golden brown. Sprinkle with red or green decorating sugar while cookies are still warm.

Dulces de Coco (Coconut Candies)

    3 cups light BROWN SUGAR
    ¼ tsp. SALT
    1 cup EVAPORATED MILK
    2 Tbsp. BUTTER
    2 tsp. VANILLA
    ⅛ tsp. CREAM OF TARTAR
    2/3 cup fresh-shredded COCONUT

In a mixing bowl, combine sugar, salt and milk. Heat over low heat until sugar is dissolved. Increase heat and cook slowly until smooth. Stir occasionally.

Remove from heat, add butter, vanilla and cream of tartar, let cool.

When cool, beat until creamy smooth. Add coconut. Mix until thick. Pour into buttered square pan, chill. Cut into squares.

Pastel de Jicama y Piña
(Jicama-Pineapple Pie)

2 cups diced, stewed JICAMA
1 cup fresh PINEAPPLE cubes
¼ cup FLOUR
1¼ cups light BROWN SUGAR
1 Tbsp. LEMON JUICE
2 Tbsp. BUTTER
dash SALT
¼ tsp. ground CINNAMON
PASTRY SHELL

In a shallow cooking pot, combine jicama and pineapple. Add flour, brown sugar and lemon juice. Blend well. Add butter, salt, cinnamon. Heat until bubbly. Cover, let simmer 15 minutes.

Make pastry shell for 9-inch pie next.

Pastry Shell

1 cup chilled FLOUR
¼ tsp. SALT
⅛ tsp. BAKING POWDER
½ cup chilled SHORTENING
2 to 3 Tbsp. ICE WATER

In a mixing bowl, combine flour, salt and baking powder. Cut in shortening, mixing each time shortening is added. Add ice water a little at a time. Make a soft dough. Form dough into a ball. Place on lightly-floured board and flatten, using a rolling pin. Roll out a circle. A thin sheet of dough should result. Place dough sheet in a 9-inch pie plate. Press down and save residual dough. Flute edge of pie plate. With remaining dough, make strips to top pie.

Preheat oven to 425 F. Fill pastry shell with jicama filling, then add strips of pastry dough to make a lattice crust. Bake in oven set at 425 F for 10 minutes, then set oven to 350 F and continue to bake for 30 minutes. Serve warm. (Makes 9-inch pie)

Kahlúa-Nut Pumpkin Pie

¾ cup BROWN SUGAR, packed
½ tsp. SALT
1 tsp. ground CINNAMON
½ tsp. GINGER
dash NUTMEG
1 EGG, slightly beaten
1½ cups canned PUMPKIN
¾ cup HALF & HALF
½ tsp. VANILLA
¼ cup KAHLUA
PECAN HALVES (enough to cover 9-inch pie)

In a mixing bowl, combine sugar, salt, cinnamon, ginger and nutmeg. Blend in egg.

Combine pumpkin and half & half. Mix well, add vanilla. Combine pumpkin mixture with sugar and spice mixture. Stir in Kahlúa, blend in well. Preheat oven to 450 F. Make pie shell next.

Pie Shell

1 cup chilled FLOUR
¼ tsp. SALT
⅛ tsp. BAKING POWDER
½ cup chilled SHORTENING
2 to 3 Tbsp. ICE WATER

In a mixing bowl, combine flour, salt and baking powder. Cut in shortening, mixing as shortening is added. Add ice water, one tablespoon at a time. Add just enough so that a soft easy dough holds.

Form dough into a ball, then lightly flour a cutting board. Place dough ball on board and flatten out, using a floured rolling pin. Work with dough until a rounded thin sheet of dough is made. Place dough sheet in a 9-inch pie plate. There should be enough dough to overlap. Even out the edge of the pie plate and remove excess dough. Leave edge of pie plain or flute edge.

Pour in pumpkin mixture. Line pie with pecan halves to cover entire surface. Bake in 450 F oven for 10 minutes. Reduce heat to 350 F and bake 35 minutes more.

Empanaditas de Calabaza (Pumpkin Turnovers)

3 cups cooked PUMPKIN, fresh
1 tsp. SALT
4 tsp. PUMPKIN SPICE
¾ cup granulated SUGAR
1 tsp. CINNAMON
dash NUTMEG

In a cooking pot, heat cooked pumpkin. Add rest of ingredients, blend in well. Bring to a bubbly boil. Cover, set aside to cool. Prepare pastry next.

Pastry for Empanaditas

2 cups chilled FLOUR
¾ tsp. SALT
2/3 cup chilled SHORTENING
4 to 6 Tbsp. cold WATER

Combine flour and salt. Add shortening, mixing evenly through flour using a baking spoon. Add water a few tablespoons at a time. Knead dough quickly and lightly until it holds together. Form 10 pastry dough balls. Do not over-manipulate dough.

Take a rolling pin and flatten out dough balls. Use waxed paper or cutting board to keep dough from sticking. Make 6 to 7-inch wide circles, add cooked filling over one side of circle. Fold over other half to cover filling completely. With a knife, cut uneven dough to smooth out half-circle. With the end of a knife or your index finger, make a seal of indentations at the end of the empanadita. Make a slit in the middle of the empanadita.

Bake at 350 F for 25 minutes or until golden brown. (Makes 10 to 12 empanaditas)

Empanaditas de Piña (Pineapple Turnovers)

1 can crushed unsweetened PINEAPPLE
8 tsp. CORN STARCH
8 Tbsp. SUGAR

In a cooking pot, add pineapple, corn starch and stir thoroughly over medium heat until corn starch is completely dissolved. Add sugar and heat, stirring frequently to keep from sticking. Cook to a bubbly boil, then set aside and let cool.   Prepare pastry next.

Capirotada #1 (Bread Pudding)

This recipe is an "old" revised recipe carried through generations. It is "topped" with panocha syrup.

BUTTER
3 EGGS, well-beaten
4 Tbsp. MILK
dash SALT
1 tsp. ground CINNAMON
¼ tsp. ground CLOVES
½ tsp. NUTMEG
2 Tbsp. light BROWN SUGAR
8 slices toasted BREAD
1 cup diced CHEESE, colby or longhorn
2/3 cup RAISINS
2/3 cup Spanish PEANUTS
¾ cup chopped PECANS (or almonds)
1 medium APPLE, peeled, cored, diced

Generously butter a square casserole dish or baking pan. Preheat oven to 375 F. In a mixing bowl, combine eggs, milk, salt, cinnamon, cloves, nutmeg and sugar. Beat until well-blended, add 1 to 2 more tablespoons milk if needed for mixing.

Place 4 toasted bread slices in buttered baking pan. Bread should fit evenly in pan. Pour half the egg mixture over the bread. Sprinkle with ½ cup cheese, raisins, peanuts, pecans and apple.

Add another layer of bread slices and repeat, using remainder of ingredients. Top entire capirotada with panocha syrup. Bake for 15 minutes until well-heated and cheese is melted. Let cool, cut into squares and serve warm. (Serves 4 to 5)

Panocha Syrup

Syrup is delicious when served over many Mexican pastries. Panocha can be made into a syrup by using water instead of milk.

2 cups light BROWN SUGAR (or 1 1/3 cup Piloncillo)
2 cups WATER

In a saucepan, dissolve sugar in water. Bring to a slow boil, stirring frequently. Cover and boil gently for 20 to 25 minutes. Spoon out any crystallized sugar that may form on the sides of the pan or over the syrup. Serve over desired pastry. (Makes 1¼ cup syrup) Store in glass jar, airtight, and refrigerate until ready to use.

Arroz con Leche (Rice Pudding)

2 cups cooked white RICE
2/3 cup WATER
1½ cups EVAPORATED MILK
½ cup MILK
pinch SALT
½ tsp. ground CINNAMON

½ cup SUGAR
½ cup RAISINS
¼ cup ALMOND slivers
¼ tsp. VANILLA
2 EGG YOLKS, well-beaten

In large saucepan, add rice and water, heat over medium flame. Allow rice to absorb all the water, then cover and put aside. In another saucepan, blend evaporated milk and milk, add salt. Bring to a slow boil until frothy. Stir constantly to keep milk from burning. Add cinnamon and sugar, mix well. Cook over medium flame, then blend in with rice. Mix well.

Let cool for a few minutes, then add raisins, almonds, vanilla and egg yolks. Mix thoroughly. Heat oven to 350 F and lightly butter a square casserole dish. Place pudding in dish, sprinkle with ground cinnamon and bake for 8 to 10 minutes, long enough to heat it. Do not leave in oven too long or rice will become too dry. When dish is warm, remove from heat and let cool a bit, then cut in portions and serve. (Serves 5)

Capirotada #2 (Bread Pudding)

8 slices white BREAD
2 to 3 Tbsp. BUTTER (or margarine)

1½ cups EVAPORATED MILK
4 tsp. GRANULATED SUGAR
2 Tbsp. light BROWN SUGAR
1 tsp. ground CINNAMON
¼ tsp. ground CLOVES

½ tsp. NUTMEG
dash SALT
¾ cup chopped PECANS
1/3 cup RAISINS
2/3 cup APPLESAUCE

Toast bread and cut into cubes. In a skillet, heat butter, then saute bread cubes in butter until bread is well-toasted. In a saucepan, heat milk but not to a boil. Dissolve sugars in milk, add all seasonings, mix in well.

Combine toasted bread cubes, pecans and raisins with milk. Stir over medium heat until bread cubes are well absorbed by the milk. Add applesauce and mix thoroughly. Place in a buttered square baking pan and chill in refrigerator for 45 minutes. Serve chilled and top with custard sauce, lemon sauce, whipped cream or topping. (Serves 4 to 5)

Cocoa Cake

The best frosting for this cake is **Chocolate Pecan** or your favorite white frosting!

> **3 cups CAKE FLOUR**
> **5 Tbsp. COCOA**
> **½ tsp. SALT**
> **3 tsp. BAKING POWDER**
> **½ cup SHORTENING**
> **1½ cups SUGAR**
> **1 tsp. VANILLA**
> **¼ tsp. ALMOND EXTRACT**
> **2 well-beaten EGGS**
> **1 cup EVAPORATED MILK**

In a large mixing bowl, combine flour, cocoa, salt and baking powder. In a separate bowl, cream shortening and sugar. Add vanilla, almond extract and eggs.

Mix dry ingredients with shortening/sugar mixture and blend well. Add milk a little at a time until it is well blended in the batter.

Preheat oven to 350 F. Butter and flour a 9-inch cake pan. Beat batter until smooth and creamy. Pour batter into pan and bake for 35 to 40 minutes or until knife comes clean from center of the cake. (Makes one 9-inch cake)

Chocolate Pecan Frosting

> **6 Tbsp. BUTTER**
> **3 squares of unsweetened CHOCOLATE, melted**
> **3 cups CONFECTIONERS SUGAR**
> **1/3 cup EVAPORATED MILK**
> **1 tsp. VANILLA**
> **½ cup chopped PECANS (or ½ cup chopped almonds)**

In a mixing bowl, cream butter, add melted chocolate and blend well. Add sugar, then milk. Add a little at a time beating well after each addition. Mix in vanilla and nuts. Whip to a creamy texture. (Makes enough for **Cocoa Cake!**)

Cochitos (Ginger Cookies)

Cochitos are part of childhood in our house. Adults, too, enjoy these rich ginger-spice cookies shaped like "pigs." Of course you can make regular drop cookies and use other cookie cutter shapes, but then they wouldn't be cochitos!

5 cups CAKE FLOUR
1 tsp. SODA
1 tsp. SALT
1 tsp. BAKING POWDER
½ tsp. ground CLOVES
1 tsp. ground CINNAMON
3 tsp. ground GINGER
dash NUTMEG
1 cup chilled SHORTENING
1 cup BROWN SUGAR (or 2/3 cup Piloncillo)
2/3 cup GRANULATED SUGAR
      (if you use Piloncillo, use ½ cup granulated sugar)
½ cup hot COFFEE
½ cup BLACK-STRAP MOLASSES
2 tsp. VANILLA

In a mixing bowl, mix flour, soda, salt, baking powder and the spices.

Cream shortening and both sugars.

Add hot coffee to molasses and blend well, add to creamed shortening mixture. Blend in vanilla.

Combine liquid and dry mixtures. Form a dough, then make a thick roll and chill thoroughly. The more chilled the dough the easier it is to cut out your cochitos!

Once dough has been adequately chilled, pre-heat oven to 350 F and bake cookies on a large, greased cookie sheet (15 minutes). (Makes 10 to 12 thick cookies, 2-inch by ½-inch)

Ginger Cake

This recipe is a variation of the **Cochito** recipe in the form of a delicious, spicy cake.

> **5 cups CAKE FLOUR**
> **1 tsp. SODA**
> **1 tsp. SALT**
> **½ tsp. ground CLOVES**
> **1 tsp. ground CINNAMON**
> **3 tsp. ground GINGER**
> **1 cup SHORTENING**
> **1½ cups DARK BROWN SUGAR (or 2/3 cup Piloncillo)**
> **2/3 cup GRANULATED SUGAR**
> **(if you use Piloncillo, use ½ cup sugar)**
> **2/3 cup BLACK STRAP MOLASSES**
> **½ cup hot COFFEE**
> **1 well-beaten EGG**
> **2 tsp. VANILLA**

In a mixing bowl, combine flour, soda, salt, cloves, cinnamon and ginger. Cream shortening and both sugars.

To molasses, add hot coffee, then mix with shortening mixture. Add egg and vanilla, mix in well.

Combine dry ingredients and molasses mixture. Make a creamy, smooth batter. Grease and flour a 9-inch cake pan. Bake at 350 F for 35 to 40 minutes, until knife comes clean from the center of the cake.

Frost with white icing or frosting. (Makes 9-inch cake)

Cream Cheese Frosting

> **6 oz. CREAM CHEESE**
> **1 tsp. VANILLA (or other flavoring)**
> **3 cups CONFECTIONERS SUGAR**

Have cheese at room temperature. Cream softened cheese with vanilla, and add sugar gradually, until mixture is of spreading consistency.

Natillas (Custard)

3 EGGS, slightly beaten
¼ tsp. SALT
1/3 cup SUGAR
3 cups scalded MILK + 2 Tbsp. EVAPORATED MILK
½ tsp. VANILLA
NUTMEG

In a bowl, combine eggs, salt and sugar. Add milk slowly, stirring constantly. Add vanilla and blend in well.

Preheat oven to 350 F. Pour custard into 6 custard dishes. Sprinkle each with nutmeg.

Place custard cups in a baking pan, add hot water up to 2/3 sides of custard cups. Bake for 30 to 35 minutes. Knife should come out clean from centers. (Serves 6) Top with sauce.

Natillas Sauce

6 to 8 Tbsp. light BROWN SUGAR
½ cup WATER
½ tsp. ground CINNAMON

In a saucepan, dissolve sugar by adding water slowly. Then add cinnamon. Heat until a smooth, clear syrup forms. Serve over custard.

Dulce de Panocha

For the sweet tooth, here is a rich brown sugar candy!

3 cups LIGHT BROWN SUGAR
2/3 cup EVAPORATED MILK
2 Tbsp. soft MARGARINE
½ tsp. ground CINNAMON
2 tsp. VANILLA EXTRACT
¾ cup coarsely-chopped WALNUTS

In a large saucepan, combine sugar, milk, margarine and cinnamon. Blend with a cooking spoon until fairly smooth. Cook for five minutes over medium heat, stirring frequently. Reduce heat to low and continue cooking for 15 minutes, stirring constantly to keep from sticking. Remove from heat and let cool for a few minutes.

When candy is no longer hot (just warm), add vanilla and walnuts. Beat in well. Butter a smooth aluminum refrigerator ice tray. Quickly spread mixture into buttered tray, as candy may harden. Cool for 25 minutes until candy has hardened and isn't so crumbly. (Makes 14 ounces of candy)

Almendrado (Almond Pudding)

Almendrado is an egg-white pudding topped by a luscious custard sauce and garnished with whipped cream and almond sprinkles. It is a traditional Mexican dessert. Layers of the pudding are tinted to represent the colors of the Mexican flag: red, white and green.

1 Tbsp. GELATIN
¼ cup COLD WATER
¾ cup BOILING WATER
1 cup granulated SUGAR

5 EGG WHITES
⅛ tsp. SALT
½ tsp. ALMOND EXTRACT
½ tsp. VANILLA

¾ cup BLANCHED ALMONDS, coarsely chopped
red and green FOOD COLORING

Soak gelatin in cold water for 5 minutes until it absorbs all the water. Add the boiling water and dissolve the gelatin. Add the sugar and dissolve it. Chill for a few minutes to set and stiffen, then beat thoroughly. Beat egg whites and add to gelatin; beat thoroughly. Add salt, almond extract and vanilla. Beat until frothy. Then mix in half the chopped almonds. Divide the mixture into three parts. Tint one red, one green and leave one white. Use a loaf pan 9 by 5 by 3. Place red mixture in first and chill to set. When stiffened, pour in white mixture, let stiffen, chill. Then add green mixture and let chill. When the almendrado is well chilled and set, top with **Custard Sauce**. (Serves 6)

Custard Sauce

2 cups MILK
5 EGG YOLKS (well beaten)
¼ cup SUGAR
⅛ tsp. SALT
2/3 tsp. VANILLA
½ tsp. ALMOND EXTRACT
¼ tsp. CINNAMON
1/3 cup finely-chopped ALMONDS
WHIPPED CREAM

In a saucepan, heat milk, add egg yolks and dissolve sugar over low heat. Add salt, blend in well. Stir until mixture thickens. When sauce is thick, let cool for a few minutes, then add vanilla and almond extract. Blend in cinnamon. Spoon sauce over almendrado, top with whipped cream and almond sprinkles. (Serves 6)

Sauce can be served individually with each serving of almendrado or over entire dessert.

Breakfast

HUEVOS RANCHEROS, p. 13
FLOUR TORTILLA, p. 21
SALSA, p. 60
Coffee/Beverage

Bowl of MENUDO, p. 35
BURRITO de HUEVO, p. 13, 14
SALSA, p. 61
Coffee/Beverage

Luncheon

CHICKEN BURRO, p. 92
REFRIED BEANS, p. 46
SALSA, p. 62
Coffee/Beverage

2 BEEF TACOS, p. 65
REFRIED BEANS, p. 46
MEXICAN RICE, p. 49
Coffee/Beverage

RED CHILI BURRO, p. 94
MEXICAN RICE, p. 49
SALSA, p. 58
Coffee/Beverage

Bowl of CALDO de QUESO, p. 37
2 CHICKEN TACOS, p. 66
REFRIED BEANS, p. 46
Coffee/Beverage

POLLO ESPECIAL, p. 86
AVOCADO SALAD, p. 44
MEXICAN CORN MUFFINS, p. 25
Coffee/Beverage

Combination Plate

BEEF TACO, p. 65
CHEESE ENCHILADAS, p. 69
SPANISH RICE, p. 49
SALSA, p. 59
Coffee/Beverage

Fiesta Plate

GREEN CHILI con CARNE, p. 95
CALABACITAS, p. 52
FRIJOLES, p. 45
FLOUR TORTILLA, p. 21
ALMENDRADO, p. 136
Coffee/Beverage

Southwest Dinner Menu

CARNE ASADA, p. 106
FRIJOLES MOLEDOS, p. 46
FIESTA HOMINY, p. 55
FLOUR TORTILLA, p. 21
SALSA, p. 58
Coffee/Beverage

Full Dinner Menu

MARGARITAS, p. 120
NACHOS, p. 29
SALSA, p. 59
CHIMICHANGA, p. 104
ARROZ con PIMIENTOS, p. 48
GUACAMOLE, p. 52
BUÑUELOS, p. 122
CAFE MEJICANO, p. 118

INDEX

T

V - Z

More Cook Books by Golden West Publishers

SALSA LOVERS COOK BOOK

More than 180 taste-tempting recipes for salsas that will make every meal a special event! Salsas for salads, appetizers, main dishes and desserts! Put some salsa in your life! By Susan K. Bollin.

5 1/2 x 8 1/2—128 pages . . . $5.95

CHILI-LOVERS COOK BOOK

Chili cookoff prize-winning recipes and regional favorites! The best of chili cookery, from mild to fiery, with and without beans. Plus a variety of taste-tempting foods made with chile peppers. 220,000 copies in print! By Al and Mildred Fischer.

5 1/2 x 8 1/2—128 pages . . . $5.95

TORTILLA LOVERS COOK BOOK

From tacos to tostadas, enchiladas to nachos, every dish celebrates the tortilla! More than 100 easy to prepare, festive recipes for breakfast, lunch and dinner. Filled with Southwestern flavors! By Bruce and Bobbi Fischer.

5 1/2 x 8 1/2 — 112 pages . . . $6.95

LOW FAT MEXICAN RECIPES

Wonderful Mexican foods, without the guilt! From low fat appetizers to savory soups, salads, main dishes, salsas and sauces, this tempting cookbook proves that low-fat *can* taste great! By Shayne and Lee Fischer.

5 1/2 x 8 1/2 — 96 pages . . . $6.95

WHOLLY FRIJOLES!
The Whole Bean Cook Book

Make beans your main dish and enjoy the benefits of their nutritious, cholesterol fighting addition to your diet. From appetizers to desserts — pintos to garbanzos, don't miss the great flavors of beans! Includes lots of bean trivia.

5 1/2 x 8 1/2—128 pages . . . $6.95

ORDER BLANK

GOLDEN WEST PUBLISHERS

4113 N. Longview Ave. • Phoenix, AZ 85014

602-265-4392 • **1-800-658-5830** • FAX 602-279-6901

Qty	Title	Price	Amount
	Arizona Cook Book	**5.95**	
	Best Barbecue Recipes	**5.95**	
	Chili-Lovers Cook Book	**5.95**	
	Chip and Dip Lovers Cook Book	**5.95**	
	Cowboy Cartoon Cook Book	**5.95**	
	Easy Recipes for Wild Game & Fish	**6.95**	
	Gourmet Gringo	**14.95**	
	Grand Canyon Cook Book	**6.95**	
	Low Fat Mexican Recipes	**6.95**	
	Mexican Desserts & Drinks	**6.95**	
	Mexican Family Favorites Cook Book	**6.95**	
	New Mexico Cook Book	**5.95**	
	Quick-n-Easy Mexican Recipes	**5.95**	
	Real New Mexico Chile	**6.95**	
	Salsa Lovers Cook Book	**5.95**	
	Tequila Cook Book	**7.95**	
	Texas Cook Book	**5.95**	
	Tortilla Lovers Cook Book	**6.95**	
	Vegi-Mex: Vegetarian Mexican Recipes	**6.95**	
	Wholly Frijoles! The Whole Bean Cook Book	**6.95**	
Shipping & Handling Add ➡	U.S. & Canada / Other countries	$3.00 / $5.00	

☐ My Check or Money Order Enclosed $

☐ MasterCard   ☐ VISA ($20 credit card minimum)

(Payable in U.S. funds)

Acct. No.   Exp. Date

Signature

Name   Telephone

Address

City/State/Zip
2/98   **Call for FREE catalog**   Mex. Fam. Favs.

This order blank may be photo-copied.